BETRAYAL

BETRAYAL OF AMERICA

Bush's Appeasement of Communist Dictators
Betrays American Principles

DAVID B. FUNDERBURK

Former U.S. Ambassador to Romania

Edited by David W. Tyson

THE LARRY MCDONALD FOUNDATION

Photographs in the Romania chapter not credited in the text are courtesy of William E. Edwards

Printed in the United States of America

Distributed by Betrayal of America
PO Box 1124
Dunn, NC 28334

Library of Congress Catalog Card Number: 91-60670

ISBN: 0-9629262-0-5 — 8.95

Other books by David B. Funderburk:
PINSTRIPES & REDS: An American Ambassador Caught Between the State Department & the Romanian Communists
BRITISH POLICY TOWARD ROMANIA, 1938-40
IF THE BLIND LEAD THE BLIND: The Mis-Teaching of Communism in American Universities

CONTENTS

ABOUT THE AUTHOR

David B. Funderburk was U.S. Ambassador to Romania from 1981 to 1985. In 1985 he resigned out of frustration with the U.S. State Department's policy of supporting Communist Dictator Nicolae Ceausescu.

Upon resigning, Ambassador Funderburk wrote a book, Pinstripes & Reds detailing the State Department's love affair with Ceausescu. Even after Funderburk left his post as Ambassador, the State Department continued to criticize him. When the overthrow of Ceausescu occurred in December 1989, the whole world realized that the State Department was wrong; and Ambassador Funderburk was right. The Wall Street Journal proclaimed that "The State Department still owes an apology to the Romanian people and to David Funderburk."

Since writing Pinstripes & Reds, Ambassador Funderburk has been warning audiences around the country that the U.S. Government, led by President Bush, is now propping up brutal dictators in China, Romania, and the Soviet Union — in the same way that Bush and the State Department helped Ceausescu.

In a February 1990 speech at the University of Colorado, Ambassador Funderburk warned of "a reckless optimism about Soviet policy" and that Gorbachev would eventually be recognized as a killer like Ceausescu was. Eleven months later, Mikhail Gorbachev ordered tanks into the Baltics—proving the Ambassador right once again.

Ambassador Funderburk's past criticism of U.S. foreign policy has proven to be deadly accurate. For that reason Americans will want to pay particularly close attention to his warnings in this book about George Bush's dangerous courtship of Communist dictators like Deng Xiaoping and Mikhail Gorbachev.

Undoubtedly, George Bush will be remembered for his stand against aggression in the Persian Gulf. But, as Ambassador Funderburk makes clear the Persian Gulf was the exception rather than the rule of George Bush's foreign policy.

Because, at the midway point of his presidency, George Bush's appeasement of Communist dictators has left him to the left of the liberal Washington Post on the issue of China, and to the left of leftist Patricia Schroeder with respect to Mikhail Gorbachev and the Baltics.

And a billion and a half people who live in those countries have been the victims of George Bush's pro-Mikhail Gorbachev and pro-Deng Xiaoping policies.

Ambassador Funderburk writes this book in hopes of bringing about change in the Bush Administration policies that are helping to keep Communist dictatorships in power in China, Romania, and the Soviet Union. So that one day, the people that live under those tyrannical regimes will be set free.

D. W. T.

FOREWORD

One of our great Presidents, Theodore Roosevelt, said "Patriotism means to stand by the country. It does not mean to stand by the President or any other public official save exactly to the degree in which he himself stands by the country. It is patriotic to support him insofar as he efficiently serves the country. It is unpatriotic not to oppose him to the exact extent that by inefficiently or otherwise he fails in his duty to stand by the country. In either event, it is unpatriotic not to tell the truth—whether about the President or anyone else."

Thomas Jefferson said,"Yes, we did pronounce a near perfect Republic, but will they keep it, or will they, in the enjoyment of plenty, lose the memory of freedom? Material abundance without character is the surest way to destruction."

I feel that God has passed out a double blessing in my life in that I have had the privilege to have known two of the greatest patriots to live in the twentieth century. The first of these, the late Congressman Lawrence Patton McDonald, gave his life for the cause of freedom. The other, David Funderburk, is giving his life to arouse the American people to the betrayal of the principles that made this the greatest country on earth.

This book will bring the readers both good and bad news. The good news is that David Funderburk has written it. The bad news is, it is true. People in high places are going to try to discredit it. Therefore, the reader should note the documentation. This book is not an opinion; it is an assembly of facts.

Thank you David Funderburk for the research and time you have put into this book. If enough people read this book, my grandchildren will live in freedom. If enough people are not awakened to what the "insiders" plans for this world are, I am afraid we will all lose our freedom. After you have read this book, join the Real Americans and help us restore America to its greatness.

Ben D. Robinson, Jr., Chairman,
The Lawrence Patton McDonald Foundation, Inc.
6240 C.R. 214
St. Augustine, Florida 32092

"The most effectual means of preventing the perversion of power into tyranny are to illuminate, as far as practicable, the minds of the people at large, and more especially to give them knowledge of those facts which history exhibits . . . ."
—Thomas Jefferson, 1779

PREFACE

I have been blessed in having a wonderful family. And I am deeply concerned about the legacy left for my children in America. Will they enjoy the fruits of liberty for which our ancestors fought and died? Or will they be subjects of a government that is Big Brother, omnipotent and intrusive?

During the 1980's I had the opportunity to serve as U.S. Ambassador to Communist Romania, and to meet with many key world figures including: the Presidents of China, Germany, Pakistan, and many other countries, Prince Sihanouk of Cambodia, Yasser Arafat, Nobel Prize Winner Elie Wiesel, etc. I visited the CIA and NSA headquarters, the Pentagon, NATO headquarters, the White House and other government offices. I had access to the highest level of top secret intelligence information. And I met two U.S. Presidents, two Vice Presidents, two Secretaries of State, two Chairmen of the Joint Chiefs, Cabinet officials, heads of the IMF, the World Bank, major corporations and banks.

I cannot—and would not—question the personal patriotism or loyalty of our elected leaders. But I can question the foreign policies of our President and State Department which can best be described as "appeasement" policies vis-a-vis major Communist tyrants. And I can observe that the Bush Administration policies are not consistent with those of our Founding Fathers but instead promote socialist government at home and the diminution of America's national sovereignty abroad.

For me to question the policies of George Bush in the wake of his great popularity from the Persian Gulf War will only subject me to more sniping and criticism from the White House and State Department (as occurred after the publication of my book Pinstripes & Reds). But in good conscience I feel that I have no choice but to help alert as many Americans as possible to the betrayal of America's principles of freedom, individual worth and dignity, and national independence by our highest government officials.

I have written this to help preserve our constitutional republic. And because it is our duty to stand with others seeking freedom from Communist tyranny. Solzhenitsyn said in his Warning to the West: "You cannot love freedom for yourselves alone and quietly agree to a situation where the majority of humanity . . . is subjected to violence and oppression."

David B. Funderburk
Buies Creek, N.C.
March 20, 1991

CHAPTER 1
BUSH'S FOREIGN POLICY TEAM

Few potential leaders in America could be more creatures of the career government bureaucracy than George Bush. He is the Insider's insider. Even a Bush adviser confessed that Bush's long experience in the federal government has left him too dependent on the bureaucracy: "he is a prisoner as well as a product of that experience." [1]

Bush believes so strongly in the wisdom of government run by bureaucratically experienced civil servants and officers, that few of his foreign policy appointments have gone to those outside the Washington establishment. And because he places so much faith in those gentlemen of wealth and power background, his administration looks largely like retreads from Richard Nixon, Gerald Ford, Nelson Rockefeller and other moderate-liberal Republican officeholders. Bush's National Security Adviser refers to his boss as a "Rockefeller Republican." [2]

Bush has long surrounded himself with fellow wealthy elitists who share a globalism view. The common bond of Bush and the Harrimans and others in the secret Yale University society Skull and Bones was "internationalism." [3] Many of Bush's closest advisers and appointees are international bankers and businessmen, or fellow oil and gas producers. His governing style tends to be secretive, and restricted to a handful of trusted advisers. One writer calls it governing by "a small elite's entitlement, the right of the political class to take care of business cozily." [4]

Bush's real liberal views have been carefully masked throughout his career. He used conservative rhetoric when it suited him in Texas politics or when running for President in 1988 on the politically popular Reagan legacy. But since becoming President, he has pushed a liberal agenda. As President, he purged the remaining conservatives and fundamentalist Christians from his

BUSH RELIES ON NIXON FOR FOREIGN POLICY ADVICE

On March 4, 1991, US News & World Report reported that Richard Nixon "is one of George Bush's most valued informal advisers. Bush speaks to - and hears from - Nixon more than he does from any other former president. White house aides say that Nixon is in contact with Bush or his senior staff virtually every month."

The following letter from Nixon to Romanian Dictator Ceausescu demonstrates Nixon's total lack of judgement about foreign leaders. This is the person Bush is relying on for advice. No wonder Bush embraces communist thugs like Deng Xiaoping. (My note to the Embassy staff reveals my thoughts about Nixon's note!)

RICHARD NIXON

January 27, 1983

26 FEDERAL PLAZA
NEW YORK CITY

His Excellency Nicolae Ceausescu:

Ever since we first met and talked in 1967, I have watched you grow in stature as a statesman. Your vigor, your single-mindedness, your acute intelligence -- and especially your ability to act skillfully on both the domestic and international fronts -- place you in the first rank of world leaders.

I say this now because when you celebrate your birthday this week you will have reached a special milestone for any leader. At 65 most people are ready to retire, but for many of the greatest leaders the most productive and satisfying years are still ahead. I am certain that your best moments will come in your second decade as President as you continue to follow the bold, independent course you have set for your people.

Mrs. Nixon joins me in sending our warmest congratulations and best wishes to you, your wife and able colleague Elena, and the rest of your family.

Richard Nixon

(COPY)

[illegible]

FYI

Anyone who could say such things about Ceausescu:

(1) doesn't know Ceausescu;

(2) must be especially grateful for getting the welcome/open door treatment in Bucharest, which is not so available to him elsewhere;

(3) must share the conviction that the accumulation, misuse and imposition of unchecked power = greatness.

return to Amb.

administration. If the proof is in the pudding, Bush's main appointments to his Cabinet and executive level positions reflect one on the left, not the one using conservative rhetoric.

Bush's attitude toward anti-communist conservatives tells much about his true beliefs. One account describes his view as an "almost pathological fear of the G.O.P.'s right wing, a phobia that dates from his start in politics." [5] Bush has "confessed" that he is "ashamed of his pandering to the right in 1964," saying he "took some of the far right positions [I] thought [I] needed to get elected" which [I] "regret" and "hope I never do it again." [6]

Bush brushed aside conspiracy believer concerns by writing in his autobiography that anti-communist conservatives in the 1960's thought "the Council on Foreign Relations was nothing more than a One World tool of the Communist-Wall Street internationalist conspiracy," and by the 1980's "they'd uncovered an internationalist conspiracy even more sinister than the Council on Foreign Relations — the Trilateral Commission." [7]

What then is this Council on Foreign Relations? The CFR is an elitist organization of power brokers from different walks of life who help promote one world government via such strategems as a New World Order. The 1989 CFR Annual Report shows that two-thirds of the over 2,500 members live in the New York and Washington areas; and that over three-fourths of the members come from business-banking, the US Government, the media and academia. [8] Most members seem to have a leftist ideology that looks favorably upon Bush's call for a New World Order. The following are representative: (media) John Chancellor, Marvin Kalb, Dan Rather; (business-banking) Dwayne O. Andreas, Nicholas F. Brady, Edgar M. Bronfman, Armand Hammer — deceased December 1990, Donald M. Kendall, David Rockefeller; and (government-politics) Lawrence S. Eagleburger, Pamela C. Harriman, Henry A. Kissinger, George S. McGovern, Claiborne Pell, John D. Rockefeller IV, and Brent Scowcroft. [9]

One can call them the insiders, the Establishment, or the CFR-Trilateralists. They always seem to put their own financial and political power interests ahead of American interests. They prefer to do business with monopoly Communist rulers. As you will see later in his book, Bush's CFR-appointees do not seek to overthrow the atheistic, secularist, Marxist-Leninist Communists in Beijing, Bucharest, or Moscow.

And George Bush has followed the CFR line. He supported the Communist monster Nicolae Ceausescu until his death. He has continued to support the butchers of Beijing even in the wake of the Tiananmen Square Massacre, and he promotes Soviet Communist Mikhail Gorbachev's program of maintaining Communist control over the captive peoples in the USSR. This is the product of a Rockefeller-Kissinger foreign policy dominated by members of the Council on Foreign Relaions who believe that the business deals of their cronies are more important than the freedom of people living under Communism.

Bush's belief in the "great man" theory of history and his reliance on those pragmatists who exclude values and beliefs from their decision-making, have led him down a blind and dangerous path.

Bush became convinced years ago of Chinese Dictator Deng Xiaoping's reform orientation and has backed the ruthless Communist boss even after Tiananmen Square.

Similarly, Bush became so convinced of Gorbachev's role in changing the Soviet Union via democratization and reform that he has continued to support Gorbachev despite all the crackdowns and repression and non-reform.

As a historian and former Ambassador, I know that great individuals have had key roles in the making of history. But that is not to say that one should exaggerate surface changes made by Deng Xiaoping and Mikhail Gorbachev; or accept every lie they utter at face value; or consider that they are somehow indispensable to world peace and America's interests.

In reality, the great foreign policy experience always touted for Bush turns out to be an experience of learning the art of appeasement, compromise, and collaboration with our greatest enemies — those who have oppressed freedom around the world. America cannot afford this.

CONGRESSMAN, 1967-1971
CHAIRMAN, REPUBLICAN NAT'L COMM., 1973-1974
DIRECTOR, CIA, 1976-1977
VICE PRESIDENT, 1981-1988
10-18-90 THE PHILADELPHIA INQUIRER
PRESIDENT, 1988-
AUTH
OUTSIDER, 1990...
THE PROBLEM IS ALL THOSE WASHINGTON INSIDERS!
DOES HE THINK WE'RE STUPID, OR WHAT?!
WHAT?
UNIVERSAL PRESS SYNDICATE

BUSH'S PRESIDENTIAL PARDON DECISIONS REVEAL HIS PRIORITIES

Nothing could tell more about George Bush's priorities as President than his Presidential Pardons.

Millions of Americans have signed petitions, written letters, and called their Congressmen requesting a Presidential Pardon for American Patriot, Lt. Colonel Oliver North. North had been a leader in the fight for freedom in Central America and around the world. President Bush refused to pardon freedom fighter Oliver North.

But in 1989 President Bush did pardon Armand Hammer — a lifelong proponent and defender of Soviet Communism. (Hammer had been convicted of illegally donating $54,000 to Richard Nixon's 1972 re-election campaign).

It is very telling that the best friend the Soviets ever had (Armand Hammer) also became a good friend of George Bush. Armand Hammer's father was a co-founder of the American Communist Party. Hammer himself was the first major American capitalist used by Lenin. Lenin told Stalin that his made-up business concession to Hammer would show that "Americans have gone in for concessions" and that it would be "a small path leading to the American business world, and it should be used in every possible way." [10]

Hammer did business with all Soviet bosses from Lenin to Gorbachev, helping steer technology and assistance to the Soviets. The Soviet Communists were and are the enemy of freedom and of America's republic.

Hammer — a member of the Council on Foreign Relations — played such a valuable role for Soviet Communist leaders both by aiding Moscow and by working to destroy the West. Hammer made billions of dollars through commercial transactions with Moscow, Beijing, and other Communist governments hostile to America. The role he played in American public and political life must have been similar to the one Lenin mapped out for him. [11] When Hammer died in December 1990, Soviet President Gorbachev described him as "an old and sincere friend of the Soviet Union who did much for Soviet-American relations and for mutual understanding between the two nations." [12]

The Arizona Republic, (a paper published for 30 years by Dan Quayle's great-grandfather and grandfather) said Armand Hammer should be remembered:

> "for sedulously helping to spread the communist malignancy through the Soviet republics and into Eastern Europe . . . wherever his ingratiating presence was useful in smoothing the way, there he was to be found, parroting the lies, collaborating with the keepers of the gulags and, always lining his own pockets . . . He sought to be on intimate terms with one of the bloodiest, most treacherous dictatorships of the 20th century . . . He knew Lenin and admired him. He found Leonid Brezhnev 'a man of great humanism and vast warmth.' When hundreds of thousands of Russians were being gunned down within earshot for resisting the Marxist nuttiness, his impulse was to keep mum and get for himself the exclusive right to export Soviet asbestos." [13]

George Bush has total faith in the State Department bureaucrats who seldom have first hand knowledge of the areas on which they provide advice. Bush has chosen to rely on the same foreign policy elite that is responsible for the greatest appeasements and the biggest sell-outs of freedom in history.

Bush has placed James Baker — a man with no prior knowledge of foreign policy — atop the State Department bureaucracy. Thus Bush has no one at the top with the knowledge to question the leftist nonsense that invariably emanates from Foggy Bottom.

A glimpse at some of Bush's most influential foreign policy advisers will make clear the values and attributes Bush holds dear. Bush's closest assistants in foreign policy and foreign trade include Secretary of State James A. Baker III, National Security Adviser Brent Scowcroft, and Deputy Secretary of State Lawrence Eagleburger.

JAMES BAKER — THE SALESMAN FOR U.S. FOREIGN POLICY

James Baker was a tennis partner of George Bush in Houston, Texas, in the 1960's. Baker like Bush attended an expensive prep school (Hill in Pennsylvania) before playing rugby and tennis at Princeton. Obviously appealing to Bush, is the fact that Baker was "born into a position of wealth, power, and status accrued through family legal, banking, and corporate interests." [14] Baker has large financial holdings in many oil companies including Atlantic Richfield, Exxon, Mobil, Standard Oil of California, and Standard Oil of Indiana.

Baker was the campaign chairman for George Bush for President. Just prior to Bush's election, Baker (who has presidential ambitions of his own) said the following:

"I know that most policy decisions are made in the Oval Office with two or three people sitting around, and I'm going to be one of those people." [15]

Baker's quote makes clear that he is interested in being in a position of power for that sake only — not for furthering the ideals of freedom.

While Baker saw to it that many of Bush's early appointments to ambassadorships "were wealthy contributors to the Bush presidential campaign who might have been otherwise unqualified," he argued the Bush Administration would do far better than most in appointing careerists." [16] Loyalty and secrecy (no leaks — something Baker has had to work on) are characteristics Baker knows Bush values.

Most conservatives remember James Baker from his days as President Reagan's White House Chief of Staff. During the early Reagan years, Baker was the chief proponent of large cuts in the defense budget. It is ironic that if the defense budget had been cut as sharply as Baker reportedly called for during the Reagan years, some of the weapons used to produce President Bush's triumph in the Persian Gulf would not have been available.

Baker is perhaps the most pro-Soviet, pro-Gorbachev member of the Bush Administration. He has carried his complete trust of the Soviets to extraordinary lengths. And his trust of the Soviets has very nearly produced some huge foreign policy disasters which will be covered in more detail in subsequent chapters.

Baker actually invited Soviet troops into Romania during the 1989 overthrow of Ceausescu — apparently oblivious to the fact that the Romanians have despised the Russians (as invaders) for centuries.

Baker invited Soviet troops to join U.S. troops in the Persian Gulf — a move that would have given the Soviets a first hand look at our weapons that we've spent billions of dollars trying to keep secret.

And it was Baker who encouraged the Soviet efforts to intervene on Iraq's behalf in the Gulf — a move that nearly let Saddam Hussein off the hook.

Baker has developed a cavalier attitude towards the truth — at times lying to the American people to cover up for Bush and for the State Department's duplicitous dealings with the Butchers of Beijing. When Baker was caught lying, he replied "I only misled them [American people] for seven days"!

That smug attitude typifies the entire foreign policy establishment that is running Bush's foreign policy.

EAGLEBURGER AND SCOWCROFT — TOP FOREIGN POLICY ARCHITECTS

The two men who actually produce the foreign policy ideas for the Bush Administration are Deputy Secretary of State Lawrence Eagleburger and National Security Adviser Brent Scowcroft. Eagleburger and Scowcroft are Kissinger proteges who in fact served as President and Vice Chairman respectively of Kissinger Associates Consulting Firm during the last four years of the Reagan Administration. Kissinger has referred to Eagleburger and Scowcroft as his "alter egos."[17]

Eagleburger and Scowcroft made from $500,000 to one million dollars annually in the Kissinger firm positions, dispensing advice and counsel to other governments — often Communist, and wiring business deals.

It was obviously financially and politically beneficial to them in this process that they had recently served various administrations in high positions with top secret security clearances and access to top secret intelligence information — political, economic, technological, scientific, and other.

Articles in The New York Times of January 24, 1989, and November 12, 1989, raise questions about the Kissinger Associates' dealings with foreign clients and many of the largest multinational companies in the world. Even though the articles raised the potential conflicts of interest, in the absence of disclosure of clients, the full list was never disclosed. [18]

Public news disclosures however showed that Kissinger Associates had as clients the Chase Manhattan Bank (Rockefellers), American Express, General Electric Company, L. M. Ericsson, and Global Motors Corporation (official Yugoslav Yugo auto company), while Eagleburger served on the boards of ITT, LBS Bank (Ljubljanska Bank of Communist Yugoslavia) and Yugo America Inc. [19] Eagleburger had earlier served as Jimmy Carter's Ambassador to Yugoslavia.

For Eagleburger to be cutting deals with Communist clients which benefitted him financially and politically was no surprise to me. I watched him for over three and one half years offer U.S. Government support and assistance to one of the world's most monstrous tyrants, Nicolae Ceausescu of Romania, in his positions as Assistant Secretary of State and Under Secretary of State. Eagleburger traveled to Romania to meet with Ceausescu and keep US-Romanian relations on a harmonious basis while Ceausescu's reign of terror and horror continued unabated (mistreated orphans, demolition of hundreds of churches and historical monuments and whole villages, etc.). He also met with Romanian Communist officials on a regular basis in Washington and Bucharest.

The Eagle or Lawrence of Macedonia (as he was known for his shoveling aid to the Communist Yugoslav region) kept the heat on me to toe the line of rewarding Communist regimes in Eastern Europe including Ceausescu's Romania. He sent an EYES ONLY cable threatening me to back off from human rights and emigration concerns in the US-Romanian relationship, so that the policy of assisting the tyrant Ceausescu could continue. Included in the warning was a completely fabricated story saying that I had passed the wrong information to the Israeli Ambassador, and that he did not know where I stood in terms of America's policy of helping Ceausescu.[20]

Overlooking what was morally right and ignoring human rights concerns, Eagleburger focused on Kissinger's global geopolitical concerns. This focus emphasized a policy of global pragmatism with personal relationships with world leaders, and making the worldwide climate safe for the major multinational corporations' acquisition of wealth and power.

Through the first four and one-half years of the Reagan Administration and now in the Bush Administration, it is Eagleburger who runs U.S. foreign policy toward the Communist world of Eastern Europe and the USSR. Eagleburger, a liberal Republican with a Masters in Political Science from the University of Wisconsin, worked for Earl Warren in his 1948 presidential campaign. In a 1986 campaign for the US Senate in North Carolina, Eagleburger gave the maximum contribution to far-left Democrat Terry Sanford (who since his election has voted 100% ADA).

Eagleburger has been described as "Kissinger's Kissinger," who was "instrumental in developing Kissinger's power base, bringing in a team of ambitious intellectuals and helping to guide his boss through the maze of Washington's foreign policy machinery."[21]

Eagleburger strongly defended Kissinger's loyalty to America when questioned in press columns by calling the attacks McCarthyite: "more than twenty years ago, as a student at the University of Wisconsin, and a member of the Republican Party, I fought Senator McCarthy because of his vicious attempt to corrupt the American political process." [22]

Eagleburger is a shrewd and cut-throat manipulator who knows where all the skeletons are located in the State Department. Eagleburger's influence in the Bush Administration is such that he chairs the committee making ambassadorial and other high level appointments. [23]

Brent Scowcroft is the other chief Kissingerite who helps formulate Bush Administration foreign policy.

Brent Scowcroft, not born into any elite, has worked through the past three decades to prove his total loyalty and confidentiality to superiors. Bush has shown his appreciation for Scowcroft's military-style loyalty and private nature, by rewarding him with the National Security position.

After working for Henry Kissinger in the government during the 1970's, Scowcroft served as Vice Chairman of Kissinger Associates (while Eagleburger was President) during the late 1980's. At Kissinger Associates, Scowcroft made in excess of $500,000 annually as a consultant for some two dozen multinational corporations and Communist Governments in Beijing, Moscow, and Belgrade.

Scowcroft apparently has blind faith in the one-world idea associated with the United Nations. In addition to his membership in the Council on Foreign Relations, he has served on the Board of Directors of the internationalist Atlantic Council, and as Vice Chairman of the United Nations Association of the U.S. [24]

For Bush to rely on Kissinger aides and proteges Scowcroft and Eagleburger for assessments of Soviet, Romanian, and Chinese Communist mind-sets is to play right into the hands of the Communists.

Bush's Ambassadorial appointees reflect the Kissinger-Eagleburger-Scowcroft mindset.

A good example is Tom Simons — Bush's Ambassador to Poland. I know Simons from first hand experience. Simons was Director of Soviet Union Affairs at the State Department while I was U.S. Ambassador to Romania. Before being named by Bush as Ambassador to Warsaw, he served as Deputy Assistant Secretary for European Affairs (includes Soviet Union).

Simons was one of the most pathetic appeasers I witnessed in the European Affairs Bureau of the State Department.

Simons groveled before Nicolae Ceausescu's brother General Ilie Ceausescu (Deputy Defense Minister) during a meeting in Bucharest, Romania. Apologizing to Ilie Ceausescu for any offense from me and Kenneth Adelman (then head of the Arms Control and Disarmament Agency), Simons assured the Communist that the Americans considered the Ceausescus good friends and would go to any length to maintain cozy relations. [25] Simons argued continually and enthusiastically for sending major assistance to the Communist Monster Nicolae Ceausescu and other East European Communist Dictators.

Simons was also a critic of President Reagan's anti-Soviet rhetoric. In his 1990 book The End of the Cold War?, Simons attacks Reagan's anti-Soviet rhetoric as "very harsh indeed." [26] The same Simons praises Gorbachev who showed very early "he was a real reformer." [27] He argues in euphoric, idealistic and some would say socialistic tones that "real convergence" between the U.S. and Soviets is ending the Cold War. [28] Now this appeaser is Bush's envoy to Poland during a critical time in its history — tailored-made for Moscow's benefit!

These are the kind of people who are running America's foreign policy. It should come as no surprise that the resulting policy is one of appeasing Communist dictators like Deng Xiaoping, Mikhail Gorbachev, and the thugs in Romania.

AP/WIDE WORLD PHOTOS

President Bush exchanges a toast with chairman Deng Xiaoping at the Great Hall of the People in Beijing. February 26, 1989

"Deng Xiaoping will 'be counted among the pre-eminent statesmen of our time.'"

— President George Bush, February 26, 1989, praising Communist dictator Deng — one of the most brutal dictators of the 20th century

CHAPTER 2

APPEASEMENT OF DENG XIAOPING — THE BUTCHER OF BEIJING:

BUSH SAYS "DENG IS ONE OF THE PRE-EMINENT STATESMEN OF OUR TIME"

MAY 20, 1989:

COMMUNIST CHINA DECLARES MARTIAL LAW

then . . .

MAY 31, 1989:

BUSH GRANTS BEIJING MOST FAVORED NATION STATUS

then . . .

JUNE 4, 1989:

COMMUNIST CHINA'S GOVERNMENT LED BY BUSH'S FRIEND, DENG XIAOPING, FIRES ON UNARMED CHINESE STUDENTS KILLING THOUSANDS OF PEOPLE

then . . .

JUNE 5, 1989- present:

BUSH LOOKS THE OTHER WAY & REFUSES TO REVOKE MFN BENEFITS FOR COMMUNIST CHINA

ITEM: TIANANMEN SQUARE MASSACRE, June 4, 1989

- Thousands killed by tanks & armored personnel carriers
- Tens of thousands arrested and many later executed
- Total crackdown on political & religious activists
- Most remaining freedoms including press snuffed out

BUSH REACTION: Business as Usual

- MFN & other trade-economic-technological benefits continue
- High level exchanges/visits continue; Eagleburger & Scowcroft go to Beijing twice; Nixon & Kissinger go to

Beijing; China's Foreign Minister and other officials meet with Bush & Baker

- Prescott Bush (George's brother) visits China on business
- Bush's Ambassador to China calls anti-Communist demonstrators "cowards"
- Bush rejects the use of sanctions

First Nixon and Kissinger and soon afterward the press and U.S. companies sold to the American people a totalitarian Communist regime in Beijing as something less than Communist. The Communist Chinese were no longer called Communists, but simply Chinese who were nationalists on the road to capitalism. They were presented as no longer a threat to the U.S. but rather an ally and counterweight to the Soviets. It was Washington which legimitized Beijing despite its legacy of tens of millions of people killed to establish Communism. David Rockefeller even described Mao Tse-Tung's accomplishments as among history's most important and successful. In the 1980's Beijing was viewed as a "benevolent dictatorship," while the supposed geopolitical value of "relations with China" took precedence over supporting freedom in China. [1]

Perhaps Bush considers himself a China hand or expert but actually Bush spent just over a year as chief of the U.S. Mission at Beijing (not embassy-ambassadorial status at that time). Following the advice and experience of Nixon and Kissinger, Bush believed that Chinese Supreme ruler Deng Xiaoping was the chief force for reform of Chinese Communism.

Apparently it never crossed Bush's mind that you cannot reform a system that is anti-family, anti-individual, anti-God, and anti-private property. Such a system is fatally flawed or irredeemable. As Alexandr Solzhenitsyn put it in The Mortal Danger: "there exist no better variants of communism, it cannot survive as an ideology without using terror and . . . consequently to coexist with communism on the same planet is impossible. Either it will spread, cancer-like, to destroy mankind, or else mankind will have to rid itself of communism." [2]

The Nixon-Kissinger-Bush policy of backing Deng Xiaoping has as an essential component the money-making opportunities for America's corporate elite — which they helped establish during the past two decades in mainland China. Kissinger in particular has personally benefitted financially (as well as politically) from his early ties to Deng. Kissinger Associates consultants (Kissinger, Eagleburger, Scowcroft) have lined up lucrative business deals for U.S. company and bank heads with Communist China — no doubt helped by their personal ties with Deng and other Chinese rulers. While the media harasses conservatives on the slightest hint of conflict of interest, the conflicts of interest of Eagleburger and Scowcroft are ignored.

Kissinger called off a foreign investment conference appearance in Beijing in September 1989 because The Wall Street Journal published an account of his business deals including his $75 million partnership called China Ventures. He was further embarrassed by Bush's sending both of his consulting firm's two top former executives to Beijing (although he of course supported the appeasement efforts in principle). Kissinger said that sending both his former executives Scowcroft and Eagleburger handed critics an opportunity "to blacken my reputation." [3]

When the Tiananmen Square massacre of tens of thousands of pro-freedom and pro-democracy demonstrators took place on June 4, 1989, the world saw the fallacy of so-called "reform communism" under Deng Xiaoping (twice Time's MAN OF THE YEAR). They also saw the utter failure of the Bush-State Department policy of sending weapons to Communist China. Despite worldwide protests and the opportunity to take the moral high ground of support for human rights, freedom and democratic development, Bush stood by his old friend Deng and his big business friends making money out of deals with repressive Communist tyrants. The Communist bosses provide monopoly business arrangements for supportive American companies, who in return backed Deng's government and turned a blind eye to the murderous repression of Beijing.

Bush continued Most-Favored-Nation status and billions of dollars in trade benefits and other economic assistance to Beijing — even after Tiananmen. In fact Bush went out of his way in official pronouncements to defend Deng. Economic or diplomatic sanctions were ruled out. No matter how he tries to rationalize it, Bush chose Communist tyrants in Beijing over those seeking freedom.

This is part of a disturbing Bush foreign policy pattern, a telling evidence of flawed Bush priorities. This may have been the best chance ever — certainly in this century —to bring some form of human rights to the one billion people of China. But once again, Bush stood on the wrong side — with the Communist totalitarian regime and against the freedom movements in China.

What does Bush's policy of support for Chinese tyrants say for his values or for those of the foreign policy establishment doing business with the butchers of Beijing?

As Vice President and President, Bush has been the foremost promoter of U.S. aid to Communist China. Beijing's repressive policies seemed to have no effect on Bush's advocacy of help for the Communists. Such help benefitted over 400 big businesses, corporations and banks, as well as individuals such as Eagleburger, Kissinger, Winston Lord (former head of the CFR and former U.S. Ambassador to China who first visited China as Kissinger's aide on his secret 1971 trip), and Scowcroft.

Mainland China continues to be one of the most totalitarian societies with the most egregious human rights violations in the world. [4] Dr. Walter Judd wrote in describing a book on China that human freedom is the central issue and "human freedom should not be brushed aside as unimportant."[5] Unfortunately George Bush has done just that.

Bush has authorized Most-Favored-Nation status, World Bank loans, and massive technology transfers for Communist China, all of which continued even after the Tiananmen Square massacre. In the past decade China has received about $10 billion in low-interest World Bank loans (40% of it interest-free). The United States is the most important member of the World Bank with Barber Conable (former liberal Republican Congressman from New York) its director. Other financial organizations like the

International Monetary Fund, the Commodity Credit Corporation, and the Overseas Private Investment Corporation, provide cheap loans, credits and other economic assistance to China and/or to U.S. companies doing business with Beijing. As is usually the case, U.S. taxpayers contributed the most money to these agencies and organizations giving China credits and cut-rate loans.

It is equally disturbing that Bush continued to grant MFN and other assistance to Communist China, even while knowing that Beijing had stolen American nuclear secrets and built a bomb with them. Beijing has the most aggressive espionage program against the U.S. currently in operation. Chinese agents stole American nuclear secrets from the Livermore National Laboratory in California and successfully produced and tested a nuclear "neutron bomb" using those secrets. [6]

Intelligence information regarding Chinese spy activities and successes in the U.S. has not prevented the President from continuing to provide high technology and weapons to Beijing. Bush continued to sell weapons and airplanes to the Chinese after the Tiananmen Square massacre. In fact, Bush said in the wake of the Tiananmen Square massacre "on the commercial side, I don't want to hurt the Chinese people." [7] Bush had no such compulsion about sanctions against South Africa and Iraq. How in the world are "the people" helped by us sending weapons to the Chinese Government for them to use against their own people? There is no real military threat to China so it's clear that the weapons will be used primarily to gun down the Chinese people and keep the "Butchers of Beijing" in power. So why are we selling them weapons?

As I learned in the Communist Romania of Ceausescu, the people are never helped by these deals. These trade concessions and the favorable publicity in being associated with the U.S. only serve to prop up the Communist regimes. It is amazing that Bush and Eagleburger seemingly didn't learn a thing from their failed policy of sending goodies to prop up Ceausescu.

The wrong signals have consistently been sent by Bush to Communist tyrants. In late February 1989, only one month after his inauguration Bush traveled to China to bolster and renew his long-standing relationship with the Communist Chinese leader. The hasty visit itself signaled Beijing that Bush was all too anxious to have a cozy relationship.

Bush's actions during his visit to China in February 1989 told the Communist Chinese dictators all they needed to know about George Bush's priorities as President.

At a February 26th dinner, Bush praised the ruthless Chinese dictator, Deng Xiaoping to the hilt saying that Deng would **"be counted among the pre-eminent statesmen of our times."**[8]

That statement must have come as a shock to the hundreds of thousands of political prisoners locked up in China by Deng Xiaoping.

And Bush went out of his way to appease the Chinese Premier Li Peng who is considered one of the hardest of the hardliners in the Chinese dictatorship. Bush "pointed out that American foreign policy in many parts of the world was under review but not China policy." [9] In other words, Bush told the Chinese that the dismal human rights record doesn't have to be improved, because Washington is going to continue to deliver economic and military assistance.

Bush met with Premier Li Peng for more than two hours. The President's spokesman, Marlin Fitzwater called the meeting "remarkable and unprecedented." Fitzwater said they talked about a wide range of topics including terrorism, the Middle East, the Korean peninsula, Chinese reforms, and missile proliferation. A wide range of topics indeed!

But did the President of the United States of America raise the question of human rights in this two-hour long meeting that, according to his spokesman covered a wide range of topics? No!

Bush's spokesman confirmed that the President did not bother to bring up human rights at his meeting with Premier Li Peng or Supreme leader Deng Xiaoping.

Asked about the importance of human rights in the U.S.-China relationship, Bush's spokesman said: "We wouldn't want to say it's the cornerstone of the relationship." [10]

Why did President Bush fail to bring up human rights in his meetings with the Chinese dictators? Quite simply, because the

Chinese dictators told him not to raise the issue of human rights.

Chinese Communist Party General Secretary Zhao Ziyang warned Bush against raising the issue of human rights. Deng Xiaoping and Li Peng also warned Bush against raising human rights questions. Li Peng told Bush that raising the issue of human rights "will cast a shadow over the good relations between the U.S. and China." [11]

So Bush kowtowed.

As one Chinese student wrote: "it is appalling — and ominous — that the new Administration was immediately intimidated."[12] Indeed, it was ominous.

Because less than four months later would come the infamous massacre in Tiananmen Square — where once again the Bush Administration would kowtow to the Butchers of Beijing.

Additionally Bush made unilateral concessions to Beijing despite China's continued repression. On Bush's return from China, Under Secretary of Commerce Paul Freedenberg announced that the shipment of thirteen categories of telecommunications, electronics, and other industrial products would be facilitated by the relaxation of export-control regulations. Speaking for the administration, Freedenberg said that "the changes reflect recognition by the U. S. and its allies of the continuing improvement in relations with China and our willingness to support improvements in China's civil sector." [13]

In April and May of 1989, most of the world cheered as Chinese students led a crusade for democracy by taking over Tiananmen Square and raising a smaller version of America's Statue of Liberty.

But the Bush Administration refused to back the brave students.

Instead of standing squarely behind the quest for freedom, Secretary of State Baker seemed more concerned about "instability" in China caused by the student protests. Baker said "I don't think it would be in the best interests of the United States for us to see significant instability in the People's Republic of China, just like I don't think it's in the best interests of the United States for us to see significant instability in the Soviet [Union]." [14] That's diplomat-speak for keeping the status quo of Communist dictatorships in both countries.

Other State Department officials — in typical and disgraceful form — openly sided with the Communist Chinese Government in its battle with the freedom-seeking students in Tiananmen Square: "The government in trouble in China is a friendly government with which we have had good relations. **We don't wish that government ill**." [15]

So there you have it, in the Bush Administration's own words — they don't want a change from the Communist government of China.

The Bush Administration's lack of support for the courageous Chinese students was so pathetic that the freedom-seeking Chinese people put more faith in Communist dictator Mikhail Gorbachev than they did in the President of the United States. As The New York Times reported on May 14, 1989: "Almost everybody seems to think that the Soviet leaders' visit to China will do more for democracy in China than Mr. Bush's trip did." [16]

The Bush Administration's statements in support of "stability" and its lack of support for the Chinese students were the ultimate acts of appeasement. And, as usual, the appeasement failed.

On June 4, 1989, the Communist dictatorship of Deng Xiaoping ("one of the pre-eminent statesmen of our time" according to Bush) brutally smashed the Chinese students. Tanks rolled in killing thousands of unarmed students. The videotape of tanks running over students outraged virtually all Americans — except the President. He was more concerned about salvaging the "relationship" with the butchers of Beijing.

After the Communist Chinese Government sent in the tanks and tens of thousands of heavily armed troops to massacre thousands of helpless Chinese students this is the honest-to-goodness reaction of the U.S. Secretary of State, James Baker:

> "It would appear that there may be some violence being used here on both sides." [17]

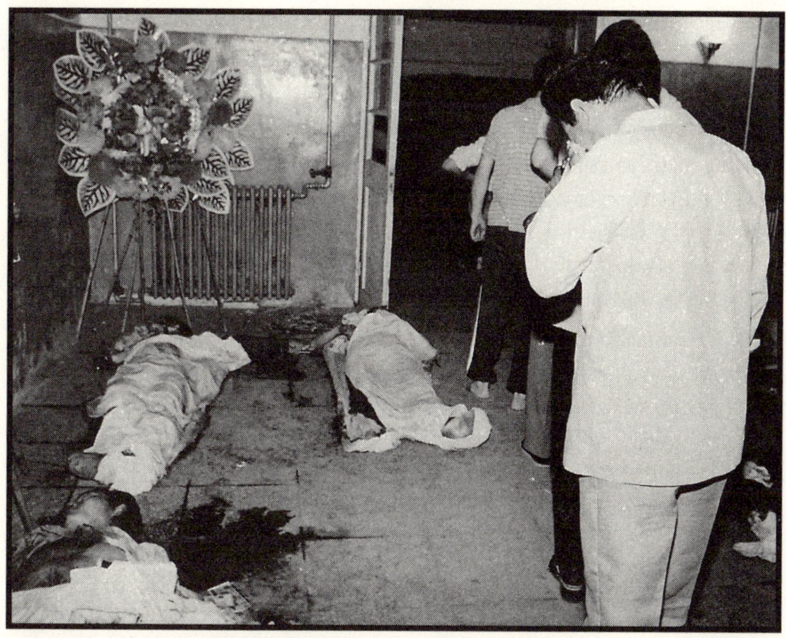

AP/WIDE WORLD PHOTOS

MASSACRE VICTIMS: Relatives and friends, covering their noses against the stench, try to identify the dead at a hospital in Beijing. June 5, 1989

Thousands, perhaps tens of thousands of students were massacred by Chinese troops — some of them run over by tanks in Tiananmen Square. Precisely three soldiers were killed. And yet the Secretary of State tries to equate the two by saying "there may be some violence being used here on both sides."

Baker's comments were an unspeakable outrage.

Bush, the man who seemingly believes every lie the Communist Chinese tell him, tried to act like his friend Deng may not have been responsible for the massacre. Even Time magazine acknowledged: Deng Xiaoping "is still China's supreme leader. He ordered the Tiananmen attack." [18]

Of course, Bush's naive and nonsensical faith in Deng's innocence was proven wrong a few days later when Deng appeared in public to praise the massacre of the students. Deng expressed no sorrow for the massacre.

And a few days later, Premier Li Peng gave his endorsement of the massacre. Li Peng, you will recall, is the man with whom Bush held the "remarkable and unprecedented" meeting only four months before. Li Peng urged that demonstrators be punished "without mercy" and he referred to the political protesters as "thugs." [19]

Congress was outraged at Bush's lack of action against the butchers of Beijing.

So finally the administration took a few meager steps.

The White House issued a statement on June 20th saying: "The President today directed that the U.S. Government suspend participation in all high-level exchanges of government officials with the People's Republic of China."[20]

While publicly saying that he had suspended high-level contacts with China, the President sent National Security Adviser Brent Scowcroft and Deputy Secretary of State Lawrence Eagleburger on a secret trip in July to appease the Chinese. This was barely a month after the massacre.

Secretary of State James Baker even lied to cover up the trip. Baker defended his deceit by saying "I only misled them (the American people) for seven days." [21]

But Bush wasn't through appeasing the Chinese. He sent Scowcroft and Eagleburger back to China in December of 1989 for a glitzy dinner. Scowcroft happily toasted the Chinese murderers as "friends" and had the gall to call critics of the massacre "irritants" to Chinese-American relations. (SEE PHOTO OF TOAST)

The Deputy Commander of the student demonstrations in Tiananmen Square, Li Lu expressed outrage at the Bush Administration visits to China in a December 1989 New York Times Op-Ed piece. He said:

> "In July before the blood was dry in Tiananmen Square, President Bush's National Security Adviser Brent Scowcroft, secretly went to Beijing to confer with the killers of Chinese students. And this month, he and Deputy Secretary of State Lawrence Eagleburger went back and danced on the grave of the Goddess of Democracy by publicly toasting China's regime. I hope that the American people and

Congress will not tolerate a foreign policy that is dipped in the blood of Chinese students." [22]

The Bush Administration's weak response to the Tiananmen Square massacre undoubtedly was seen by Deng as a green light to continue repression even after the massacre.

According to the Chinese student leader Li Lu, "Hundreds of thousands were arrested; many were tortured. Amnesty International has documented secret executions, perhaps as many as 10,000 since June 4" — the date of the Tiananmen Square massacre. [23]

The U.S. should never grant MFN treatment to a government engaged in systematic human rights abuses and imperial repression. Similarly the U.S. should solidify relations with the free Republic of China on Taiwan. One should not reward enemies for dastardly acts while pulling the rug out from under our true friends and allies.

Bush has been so crass in his lack of concern for human rights abuses in China that he has even been severely criticized — and rightly so — by the left wing Democrats and media. Senate Majority Leader George Mitchell's votes have ranked him 95% by the liberal ADA and AFL-CIO. [24] And even Mitchell accused Bush of "embarassing kowtowing" to the butchers of Beijing. [25] House Majority Leader Richard Gephardt who has become as liberal as Mitchell in his votes, called Bush to task for his veto of legislation that would have allowed Chinese students on expired visas to extend their stays in the U.S. for another four years. Gephardt called Bush's veto "a tragic error," which put 32,000 students' lives at risk.[26] It is sad when a Republican President goes so far in appeasing Communists that liberal Democrats find it repugnant.

Bush had previously said that: "when you see these kids struggling for democracy and freedom, this would be a bad time for the U.S. to withdraw and pull back and leave them to the devices of a leadership that might decide to crack down further." [27] Haiching Zhao of the Independent Federation of Chinese Students and Scholars said following the Bush veto that "China's despots know that they can dictate how the U.S. government responds to their

A CHINESE STUDENT LEADER SAYS BUSH BOWS TO BEIJING BUTCHERS

"I was the deputy commander of the student demonstrations in Tiananmen Square. Last April, May and June . . . army tanks and guns killed and wounded thousands. Hundreds of thousands were arrested; many were tortured. . . Yet in July, before the blood was dry in Tiananmen Square, President Bush's national security adviser, Brent Scowcroft, secretly went to Beijing to confeer with the killers of Chinese students. And this month, he and Deputy Secretary of State Lawrence Eagleberger went back . . . publicly toasting China's regime. Our hopes in Tiananmen Square were built on the principles that frame the U.S. Constitution and Bill of Rights. . .Why has the Bush Administration left us in the cold? . . . I hope that the American people and Congress will not tolerate a foreign policy dipped in the blood of Chinese students."

Li Lu
New York Times, December 24, 1989

AP/WIDE WORLD PHOTOS

Beijing citizens yell oaths against the government as they gather around the body of a man killed by an armoured personnel carrier on its way to Tiananmen Square. June 4, 1989

AP/WIDE WORLD PHOTOS

U.S. National Security Adviser Brent Scowcroft, right, raises his glass in a toast with Chinese Foreign Minister Qian Qichen during a banquet welcoming Scowcroft and Eagleburger to Beijing. December 9, 1989

repression of the democracy movement." [28] A Washington Post editorial of mid February 1991 attacked Bush's "sorry record" on China in the wake of Tiananmen Square. [29]

Bush has obviously put the maintenance of "good" relations with Beijing (the geopolitical Realpolitik concerns of Henry Kissinger) ahead of human rights concerns. Kissinger's efforts to appease Beijing (after Tiananmen) went so far as to condemn the student's demonstrating for democratic government and to defend Deng's murderous actions.[30] When former President Richard Nixon and Kissinger returned from exploratory trips to China with the news that the Chinese Communists sought closer ties but preferred for the U.S. to make the first moves, Bush considered the time to be right.[31]

Then he sent Eagleburger and Scowcroft on the "secret" mission before the blood from Tiananmen Square had even dried. The actions and words of Eagleburger and Scowcroft in friendly toasts to Deng and in putting the onus on the critics of the massacre as "irritants" to Sino-American relations were in fact embarassing kowtowing to the Beijing Communists. [32]

GAMMA LIAISON

Scowcroft & Eagleburger meet with Chinese Premier Li Peng, after the Tiananmen Square massacre, behind which Peng was a prime mover. Peng said student demonstrators should be punished "without mercy." December 14, 1989

In late December 1989, Bush dispatched Scowcroft on a second mission to Beijing which was headlined as "Hailing the Butchers of Beijing" in a New York Times editorial.[33] Bush himself in an interview with U.S. News & World Report said "I'm confident there will be changes that are recognized as steps toward — be careful how I say this — but steps toward the values of openness we treasure." [34] Over a year later and the world is still waiting for these changes in China.

More recently, Bush continued the appeasement by extending Most Favored Nation status and by renewing his own personal contacts. On May 25, 1990, Chinese Prime Minister Li Peng thanked Bush for renewing MFN (the first time it came up for extension after Tiananmen). On June 4th, the anniversary of Tiananmen, Bush "appeared to go out of his way to avoid language that might be offensive to Beijing or jeopardize the conciliatory policy that he adopted last year, a policy criticized by many in Congress as not forceful enough."[35] On November 30, 1990, Bush hosted the Chinese Foreign Minister Qian Qichen in Washington and assured him that "we have many things in common." [36]

The Persian Gulf War allowed Bush to continue his policy of ignoring human rights abuses in China. Left-wing columnist Mary McGrory described Beijing as "Mr. Bush's favorite totalitarian dictatorship" where its MFN status remains untouched. [37] The case that aroused the ire and attention of McGrory and others is that of the Western media's leading Chinese dissident Fang Lizhi.

Fang has spoken out about America's double standard on human rights. He has pointed out the five-year prison sentences given to some of the Tiananmen Square demonstrators in February 1991, and of those others who have not even received the charade of a trial. Fang has reported that many dissidents have been sent to the approximately 1,000 labor reform camps where 50,000 to 80,000 people are held captive. Fang has been praised by many humanitarian groups, but not received by George Bush.[38]

On February 12, 1991, it was announced that Wang Juntao and Chen Ziming received 13 year prison terms for their involvement in the 1989 pro-democracy demonstrations. The harsh sentences were part of the trials being carried out by Beijing during the Persian

HOW THE BUSH POLICY OF REWARDING THE CHINESE COMMUNISTS HAS HURT THE AMERICAN ECONOMY SINCE THE TIANANMEN SQUARE MASSACRE:

U.S. IMPORTS OF CHINESE GOODS "ROSE BY 40% IN 1989 AND BY 35% IN 1990, [BRINGING] CHINA'S ESTIMATED EXPORTS TO THE U.S. TO AT LEAST $16 BILLION AND MAYBE MORE.

THE RESULT: A U.S. TRADE DEFICITWITH CHINA OF $11.5 BILLION . . . EXCEEDED ONLY BY THE $41 BILLION DEFICIT WITH JAPAN.

UNTIL 1983 THE U.S. HAD HAD A TRADE SURPLUS WITH CHINA."

SOURCE: FORTUNE, MARCH 25, 1991

Gulf War and described as "rough justice in Beijing" by the U.S. based human rights organization known as Asia Watch. [39]

The same Deng Xiaoping hailed by Bush, Nixon and Kissinger as "among the pre-eminent statesmen of our time" remains a crusher of freedom. In mid-February 1991, Deng warned Hong Kong that: the anti-Beijing party which supports democracy in China "has to be kicked out of the political establishment . . . If they create turbulence . . . If there is a major rebellion, the central government has to send troops."[40] Deng went on to say that things will not change with time because "I'm confident that the core leadership of the third and fourth generations formed after we, the elders, die will insist on socialism . . . Some people in Hong Kong should not have too many unrealistic illusions." [41] There it is from the horse's mouth.

In his policy of rewarding Deng Xiaoping and the Communist Chinese, Bush has relied on his own personal experience and connections, and on the Kissinger-Eagleburger-Scowcroft (Kissinger Associates) group, James Lilley (current U.S. Ambassador to Beijing and Bush friend), and Richard Nixon.

Bush's disdain for the pro-freedom forces in China is visible in the man he appointed to be U.S. Ambassador to China — James Lilley. Lilley impressed Bush with his "intelligence" reporting in Beijing when Bush was stationed there from the fall of 1974 through 1975 (13 months) and Bush rewarded Lilley by appointing him U.S. Ambassador to China in 1989. In December 1990, while escorting the Chinese Foreign Minister (the official foreign spokesman for the butchers of Beijing) around Seattle, Lilley placed the Bush Administration squarely against the human rights supporters by criticizing anti-Beijing demonstrators as "cowards" and telling one protester "to go back to China and serve China." [42]

Why would someone who had spent time in China not understand the horror of totalitarian Communism's effect on the people? It might have helped if he had lived with a Chinese family. Perhaps Bush did not know Chinese and did not see the extent of the repressiveness? Or perhaps he knew of it from intelligence reports and became convinced that supporting so-called reform communists like Deng Xiaoping was the best policy for America.

While serving as the U.S. Ambassador to Romania I read intelligence information about the miserable situation in China and I met Chinese officials in Bucharest. I had studied about Chinese Communism under Professor Richard L. Walker at the University of South Carolina. Walker was the author of a Senate Judiciary Committee Study The Human Cost of Communism in China, an account which catalogs human deaths which may total as high as 64 million attributed to Communism in China. [43] The Deng Xiaoping regime obviously has some of this blood on its hands, and in fact has continued to kill political and religious opponents of the regime. Deng himself said just before Tiananmen "we do not mind spilling a little blood." [44]

How can any believer in religious and political freedom and individual worth and dignity favor assisting such a regime? Only in the context of helping over 400 wealthy businessmen and bankers and helping carry out a policy leading toward one world government can one understand such a policy. But what is best for the Council on Foreign Relations elite and one world government is not best for the Chinese people or for America's image. The damage to America's moral image from supporting the butchers of Beijing in the wake of Tiananmen Square and the killing of pro-democracy demonstrators has been ignored.

The essence of the Bush Administration policy of appeasement is how it has encouraged the Chinese Communists to further repress the people. Albert Jolis, executive director of The American Foundation for Resistance International, has best expressed the failure of Bush-Baker diplomacy: "eleven days after . . . China declared martial law (May 31, 1989), President Bush granted that country Most Favored Nations Status, and exactly three days after that, the Chinese government drove its tanks into the unarmed students on Tiananmen Square." [45]

POLICY RECOMMENDATIONS:

- No MFN or economic benefits of any kind should be granted to a regime that violates all fundamental human rights and kills its own people (who oppose them)
- No high level visits by U.S. officials should be sent to China or received in the U.S. while individuals are jailed on accusations of opposition to the state
- The U.S. Government should make it known in the strongest possible terms that Beijing's massacre violates all norms of civility and that we cannot be friends of such a regime
- The U.S. Government should make it clear that we support those struggling for freedom from tyranny

AP/WIDE WORLD PHOTOS

Bush courting Gorbachev at the White House. May 31, 1990

CHAPTER 3
THE REAL GORBACHEV:
"I AM A CONVINCED COMMUNIST"

"perestroika is no retreat from Communism but rather a step toward the final realization of Marxist-Leninist utopia; a continuation of Lenin's ideas. Those who expect us to give up communism will be disappointed."

— Mikhail Gorbachev to the Politburo, November 1987

" . . . there is no greater advocate of perestroika than the President of the United States."

— George Bush, speaking to the American people, November 22, 1989

Yuri Andropov, the butcher of Budapest, who ordered tanks to kill thousands in Hungary in 1956, was later the KGB chief in Moscow. Andropov groomed Mikhail Gorbachev for power in the Soviet Union. And Andropov's successor as KGB head, Viktor Chebrikov, was Gorbachev's ally in his accession to power.

In 1985, Mikhail Gorbachev — orthodox Communist — came to power.

Since then, an elaborate propaganda and public relations campaign, has made Gorbachev the West's hero and superman. The U.S. and West have always preferred to believe the illusion that freedom and peace are easy and free. And the West believing that Gorbachev meant what he said (or what was projected about him via disinformation), was convinced that Gorbachev could do no wrong. Our President rushed to have huge "summits" with Gorbachev because he is such a media star.

George Bush's romancing of Mikhail Gorbachev has been the silliest spectacle in American foreign policy since Jimmy Carter kissed Leonid Brezhnev.

We were told by the foreign policy establishment that Gorbachev was the prime mover behind freedom in Eastern Europe; that Gorbachev alone allowed the development of an internal economic reform program known as perestroika; that Gorbachev allowed the U.S. to get resolutions condemning Iraq in the United Nations and was working with us in the Persian Gulf; and that Gorbachev was allowing democratization in the Soviet Union through glasnost.

The old Bolsheviks finally found the ideal front man to win over the West while they continue to carry out their objectives and even use many of the same tactics: Mikhail S. Gorbachev. [1]

The decision of Moscow to market Gorbachev (Madison Avenue PR-like) to the U.S. and West like any other product was a brilliant move. It has worked almost to perfection, with Gorbachev now perceived by a majority in the West as a good Communist (if even a Communist at all) with good policies (glasnost and perestroika), and good intentions. Time's Man of the Decade and Nobel Peace Prize Winner can do no wrong in Western eyes. He is the good guy fighting against the bad guys in the USSR to save glasnost and perestroika.

As a result, George Bush has even been sending financial assistance to the Soviet Union when the U.S. entered a recession. Bush even raised the taxes of middle income Americans to do it. Look at all the "goodies" Bush has sent to Gorbachev:

- Bush has recommended Most Favored Nation Status for the Soviet Communists, which opens the door for all kinds of aid.
- Loans, credits, and business insurance for Moscow were recommended through the vehicles of the U.S. Export-Import (Ex-Im)Bank, the Overseas Private Investment Corporation (OPIC), and the Commodity Credit Corporation (CCC).

- Up to $300 million in credits from the Ex-Im Bank can be given Moscow for the purchase of thousands of computers from IBM and for other high tech items.
- $360 million was pledged to the European Bank for Reconstruction and Development, which will give reduced rate loans to the Soviets.
- $12 billion was pledged to the World Bank, which will grant cheap loans to the USSR.
- Billions of dollars in subsidized grain sales to Moscow have already been made to Gorbachev by Washington.
- Bush proposed a special association for the Soviets with the International Monetary Fund (IMF) and the World Bank.[2]
- Hundreds of millions of dollars in food assistance has been sent to the Soviet Union chiefly to boost Gorbachev's positions, despite the fact that humanitarian need is greater elsewhere, and the fact that the Soviets have billions in foreign exchange and just had one of their greatest harvests ever. [3]

The foreign policy establishment bought lock, stock and barrel this notion of Gorbachev the Great — reformer, democrat, liberalizer, liberator, Man of the Decade if not century, Nobel Prize Winner! When Gorbachev won the Nobel Prize, the Bush Administration actually praised Gorbachev's selection.

In their rush to embrace Gorbachev, George Bush and the State Department ignored the consistent aspects of Gorbachev's rule that were no different than his predecessors:

- the steady accumulation of titles and personal political power for Gorbachev exceeding even that of Joseph Stalin;
- the bullying and repression of the Baltic states after they had declared independence;
- the bloody repression of Georgians and Armenians and others who demonstrated against the state;
- the Gorbachev support for mutilation bombing of Afghan

children and women;
- the continuation of Soviet espionage and disinformation campaigns worldwide;
- the continuation of power centered in the KGB, the military and the Communist Party bureaucracy (nomenklatura);
- the resignation of Eduard Shevardnadze as Soviet Foreign Minister in December 1990 and his warnings of Gorbachev's full-scale movement toward dictatorship.

We are told by the State Department that we need the well-intentioned Gorbachev, to help us in the United Nations, in the Persian Gulf, to maintain world peace, to maintain stability in the Soviet Union. Gorbachev is good, even a baptized Christian we are falsely told. It is the hardliners in the Politburo, in the military, in the KGB, and in the Communist Party, who are forcing Gorbachev to become more dictatorial, we are led to believe. If only we support Gorbachev during his dire moment of crisis and need, we can prevent instability and chaos and the violent overthrow of the Moscow government.

I should add that through the years of the Cold War we thought we were defending the Judeo-Christian values of the West and America's constitutional republic against the "evil empire" of the Soviet Union.

Now we are supposed to rush economic and financial assistance to help save the Communist system we have been fighting during the past decades. President George Bush proclaims that it is in America's best interests to save the Communist dictator Gorbachev and the Communist system in the Soviet Union. When the Soviets had one of their largest grain crops in history in 1990, we rushed them food assistance.

If the Soviets are in such dire straits — and I hope they are — why don't we simply tell them to stop sending billions of dollars in aid to Communist Cuba and Afghanistan and use the money at home. Secondly, if the Soviets need more money for food they can take the money from their bloated defense budget, not the taxpayers of the United States. The taxpayers of the United States didn't cause the food shortages in the Soviet Union; their Communist system backed by the military did. So why not let them pick up the tab?

George Bush has asked the American people to believe that Gorbachev was first a democratic reformer and liberator and now under pressure from others is becoming a dictator. I still believe that orthodox Communist Gorbachev in 1985 is still an orthodox Communist Gorbachev in 1991.

Why does President Bush try to tell the American people that Gorbachev is a proponent of democratic reform when Gorbachev himself says: "I am a convinced Communist."?

Why is Bush trying so hard to make us believe in this elaborate charade (sending aid and trade) which does not benefit the American people or the people in the USSR and Eastern Europe who believe in and fight for freedom and democratic government?

Why does Bush insist on helping Gorbachev and the Communists in the USSR, in the same way that he helped the Communists in mainland China and in Romania under Ceausescu?

Because of Soviet propaganda and statements and actions by Bush and the State Department, the majority perception in America is that Communism is dead, Eastern Europe and the USSR are free and developing democracies and free enterprise economies, and the Cold War is over. Gorbachev is the reformer, liberator, democratizer and peacemaker. And we have won the Cold War.

What we have not been told by the major media and the State Department is what Gorbachev's intentions and plans have been; what actions have been taken by the Soviet Communists to maintain power and control; and how a gullible (or deliberate) U.S. policy is preventing the development of real freedom in Eastern Europe, the USSR and China.

George Bush completely bought into the Gorbachev Is Good Myth and has said (January 1990) "I want very much for him [Gorbachev] to succeed," and (November 1989) "there is no greater advocate of perestroika than the President of the United States."

But the people who have lived under Communism in the Soviet Union know the real Gorbachev (polls in the USSR have given Gorbachev only 15-20% support), and they understand how Bush's policies play into the hands of the Communists.

Elena Bonner, widow of Nobel Peace Prize Winner and leading Russian dissident Andrei Sakharov, predicted the following about Gorbachev:

> "[Gorbachev] inspires utmost distrust... and may well pass into history not as the architect of perestroika but as the architect of genocide." [4]

> Bonner warned the West about placing its trust in Gorbachev:

> "It took 70 years to destroy the myth of socialism . . . but eliminating . . . its [socialism's] harmful consequences . . . will be complicated by the birth of a new myth — that Gorbachev is striving for democracy in the face of opposition and that the only way to help him is by silence in the Soviet Union and in the West."[5]

Gary Kasparov, World Chess Champion and founder of the Democratic Party in the USSR, puts the blame for helping Gorbachev and other Communists stay in power squarely on Bush and other Western leaders:

> ". . . the current American President is one of the architects of this policy [support for the Chinese Communists], and his failure to blame the Chinese Communists for the bloodshed in Tiananmen Square is another grave mistake. And now we see a similar mistake happening in the Soviet Union. We see Western governments prepared to offer huge economic support, some $18 billion, to the current Communist regime . . . If we look back over the history of Communism, we must admit that for the past 73 years, Communism was able to exist only because of the mistakes made by the West. The West admired Lenin. The West admired Stalin. The West admired Khrushchev. The West admired even Brezhnev. And now the West admires Gorbachev ... For us who are fighting against Communism inside the country and attempting to promote Western style

> democracy. . . How can we explain why the West persists in giving such enormous economic aid to a dying regime? Of course we cannot do it. I beg you to think about the future." [6]

Vladimir Bukovsky, President of Resistance International and leader of Russian Democratic groups in the West, points out how Western help for Gorbachev goes against the true aspirations of the people in the USSR:

> "The West has consistently made the mistake of ascribing 'good intentions' to Gorbachev . . . The West, moreover, has utterly failed to comprehend . .. [the people] share the same burning hatred of communism in all its forms . . . The Soviet people do not want a reformed communist system . . . Recent food supplies alone strengthen Gorbachev's position considerably since they are channelled exclusively through the central government. The refusal of the West to recognize the independence of the Baltic republics, and its lukewarm expressions of sympathy for the national movements as such is no less important than all the billions of dollar credits showered on him."[7]

But the Bush Foreign Policy Team still insists on doing everything it can to save Gorbachev and his Communist system and develop the "New World Order."

The Soviet record of the past 74 years is the best basis for determining whether we should trust Gorbachev's promises and prop him up. In brief, the record of the Soviet Communists includes the destruction of over 80% of the churches that ever existed; the killing of over 50% of the clergy; and the deaths of over 40 million people (a figure even acknowledged by the Soviet Government in 1990). A lot of this was done to forcibly communize, collectivize, nationalize and maintain power for an atheistic elite of Marxist-Leninists. Should anyone trust the leaders (Gorbachev et al) of a regime responsible for such a criminal legacy? Even if they have a nice smile? Of course not.

Vitaly Korotich, Russian Parliamentarian and journalist, put it this way: *"more than 40 million have been killed in our country from the time of the October Revolution. If each one of those people were to receive one minute of silence — that would amount to more than 73 years of silence: the time that has passed from the Revolution until now* (italics mine)." [8]

So what does Mikhail Gorbachev have to say about the Leninist record of massacring 40 million people in the USSR? Gorbachev wrote in his book Perestroika that "we have always learned, and continue to learn, from Lenin's creative approach to the theory and practice of socialist construction," and that " . . . the works of Lenin and his ideals of socialism remained for us an inexhaustible source of dialectical creative thought, theoretical wealth and political sagacity. His very image is an undying example of lofty moral strength, all-round spiritual culture and selfless devotion to the cause of the people and to socialism. Lenin lives on in the minds and hearts of millions of people." [9]

Gorbachev has long claimed to look to Lenin for answers and wrote in Perestroika that his "thirst to know him [Lenin] more extensively in the original grew," as his "interest in Lenin's legacy."[10]

Indeed, Soviet objectives and Gorbachev's intentions are not as noble as George Bush and company would have you believe. It was never Gorbachev's intention to liberate Eastern Europe from Communism, but rather to allow the discredited hardline rulers (Kadar in Hungary, Honecker in East Germany, Zhivkov in Bulgaria, and Ceausescu in Romania) to be replaced by Gorbachev Communists with so-called human (reform) faces like Iliescu in Romania. He felt these "good Communists" could possibly mollify their people and stay in power. He did make the fateful decision not to use troops and tanks to keep the Stalinists in power in Eastern Europe , but his real intention was to project surface reform changes without real reform or without really undermining Communist Party domination and power.

Gorbachev also wanted to get the West to bail out and rebuild Eastern Europe which Communism helped bankrupt and devastate. Part of Gorbachev's predetermined strategy was apparently to help salvage the Communist system by getting a massive influx of assistance from the West. [11] Also the Soviet plan included a condominium for Central and Eastern Europe in which Western financial investment and high technology rebuild the area while it remains under the military dominance of Moscow. [12] And the West may be participating in yet another version of Yalta by abandoning the interests of Central and East Europeans in exchange for "promises" by Moscow to "behave differently." [13]

While Gorbachev has been sold as a reformer, democrat, liberator and peacelover, his own words are quite different. In his book Perestroika, Gorbachev says: "perestroika is no retreat from communism but rather a step toward the final realization of Marxist-Leninist utopia; a continuation of Lenin's ideas. Those who expect us to give up communism will be disappointed." [14]

Gorbachev also reportedly said to the Politburo in November 1987: *"comrades do not be concerned about all you hear about glasnost and democracy. These are primarily for outward consumption. There will be no serious internal change in the USSR other than for cosmetic purposes. Our purpose is to disarm America and let them fall asleep. We want to accomplish three things — (1) the Americans to withdraw conventional forces from Europe, (2) the Americans to withdraw nuclear forces from Europe, and (3) the Americans to stop proceeding with the SDI* (italics mine)." [15] Gorbachev forgot to mention that he also wants the economic and financial bailout of the Soviet economy (as well as the East European economies) by the West.

Gorbachev has stated on many occasions his admiration for Lenin, that he is a Leninist, and that he considers Lenin's actions at Brest-Litovsk to be a proper model for today. At the Treaty of Brest-Litovsk in 1918, Lenin was willing to make large concessions in order to preserve the Bolshevik Revolution and Communism. Tens of millions of people and huge chunks of territory were given up by Lenin during the temporary retreat, as compromise was considered a weapon to be used to pursue the main goal. As Gorbachev put it: "Lenin was right . . . [Lenin's retreat at Brest-Litovsk] proved the strength of Marxist-Leninist dialectics." [16]

Thus Gorbachev praised Lenin's tactical retreat to gain breathing space or time to renew the offensive later. It should also be kept in mind that Gorbachev's idol Lenin wrote in a letter to the Politburo on March 19, 1922: "the more representatives of the clergy we manage to shoot the better — now is the time to teach the lesson that for many decades the people will not dare even think of resistance." [17]

People in the Soviet Union have not forgotten Lenin's legacy. And America should not forget that Gorbachev is the very willing heir to Lenin's legacy.

Gorbachev has even employed tried and true Leninist tactics. The Soviet Communists have throughout their history tried to use other left-wing groups as well as "useful idiots" in the West to show their willingness to compromise and make concessions. Lenin considered any tactic justifiable to bring about Communist victory, and Lenin said "Communist morality is based on the struggle for the consolidation and completion of Communism." [18]

The coalition tactic was used by the Soviets to set up Communist front governments throughout Eastern Europe in the wake of World War II. Soon the Communist front or coalition governments were solely Communist. Similarly Moscow has used the tactic of isolating those strong, principled anti-communists who have refused to compromise or collaborate in any way with Communists. In post-World War II Eastern Europe most of these courageous figures were executed by order of Moscow.

Today the Baltics provide a prime example. Gorbachev has used tried and true Soviet methods to "isolate" a strong leader of freedom, independence, and democratic government, Lithuania's President Vytautus Landsbergis. Gorbachev drew the distinction between Landsbergis who refused to compromise and the Latvian and Estonian leaders who were more willing to compromise with Moscow.

Lithuania also constitutes the biggest problem for Moscow because of its overwhelmingly ethnic Lithuanian and deeply religious population. Thus wedges have been deliberately driven by Moscow between the Latvian-Estonian Governments on the one hand and the Lithuanian Government on the other. In all Baltic states Gorbachev has used the shadowy Soviet puppet organizations of the Communist Party (called National Salvation Committees or

Fronts). Note that the committee in Lithuania is called the National Salvation Front just like in Romania.

During the war in the Persian Gulf region, Bush declared that we were there to bring about the New World Order with the Soviets via the UN, and to resist aggression. It was okay for the Soviets to crush the Latvians and Lithuanians, but not for Iraq to crush Kuwait.

Just as Bush did with the Chinese Communists after Tiananmen Square, he conducted a blatant policy of appeasement vis-a-vis the Soviet killings in the Baltic states in January 1991. Instead of halting plans to give full-scale aid to the Soviets, Bush continued with business as usual. His paramount concern was to maintain the new cozy relationship with the dictator Gorbachev at all costs.

Bush has gone out of his way to believe Gorbachev at face value even when others urged caution. Some Bush advisers advised Bush not to rush to assist him just as he was cracking down and using troops against the Baltic peoples, but Bush naively trusts Gorbachev because he has talked to Gorbachev face to face. [19]

The extent of Bush's appeasement of Gorbachev is almost unbelievable. To appease Gorbachev, Bush did the following:

- Bush abandoned a five decades-old policy of not recognizing the forcible incorporation into the USSR of Estonia, Latvia, and Lithuania;
- agreed to give five strategic Alaska islands to Moscow in a totally concessionary new agreement;
- approved technology transfers for the Kama River truck factory (the very truck factory that produced the trucks that went into Afghanistan) while the Soviets still send massive aid to the Afghan Communists ($300 million per month);
- agreed to military concessions to Moscow in order to get a START treaty of dubious value even as evidence was widespread of Soviet violations of the INF Treaty;
- pledged billions of dollars to Moscow in grants, credits, loans, trade benefits, and subsidized loans from U.S.[20]

All of this assistance was granted to Moscow by Bush even though evidence was increasing of a crackdown and repression. Bush even made apologies for Gorbachev's dictatorial actions and continued grab for political and economic power. As Bush put it: "any time you move from a totalitarian, totally controlled state to an open state . . . perestroika in terms of reform, glasnost in terms of openness, you are bound to have problems." [21]

The Bush aid to Gorbachev was widely projected as an effort to "ensure the political survival of Soviet President Mikhail Gorbachev by helping him maintain stability." [22]

Everyone schooled in Marxist-Leninist terminology knows that order and stability are code words for dictatorial crackdowns and repression. Bush stated that his aid initiatives to Moscow were designed to further the goal of "the Soviet Union [playing] a role as a full and prosperous member of the international community of states." [23]

Frank Gaffney of the Center for Security Policy (and former member of Reagan's NSC) said: "it is astounding that President Bush would act to waive the Jackson-Vanik Amendment tying preferential treatment to Soviet respect for human rights in the midst of mounting evidence of an imminent and probably bloody crackdown" (this turned out to be accurate), and that it is the best proof to date that Bush "favors the appearance of 'stability' offered by repressive regimes over the often untidy but indispensable exercise of human rights, political freedoms, and economic opportunity by democratic forces in the USSR and elsewhere." [24]

Again, how could anyone (Bush included) consider Gorbachev and Soviet Communism to be real friends of American liberty? Why would Bush extend such aid to a Communist regime engaged in increasingly tyrannical actions? This would not make sense if Bush were not dedicated to carrying out plans for the New World Order which would protect and enhance the financial-economic assets of his Insider cohorts.

The limits of glasnost were recently shown when Izvestia's plans to report new details of the Soviet downing of Korean Air Lines (KAL) 007 were killed by the Soviet Government.

Izvestia planned to reveal sensational details based on interviews with eyewitnesses and secret government sources, which would shed light on what truly happened to the airplane and passengers and crew in 1983.

According to leaked details from Izvestia, KAL 007 (contrary to official Moscow statements) crashed off the Soviet Pacific island of Moneron and remained largely intact at a depth of approximately 100 feet. In order that the discovery of the plane would be kept secret, the Soviet Government had the bodies of the 269 victims cremated in a local crematorium. [25]

They also learned that electronic gear aboard the plane showed — again contrary to Soviet Defense Ministry propaganda — that the plane had accidentally veered off course and was not on a spy mission. Soviet officials covered up these facts in order to hype propaganda that the United States was about to launch a nuclear attack on the Soviet Union. [26] On Gorbachev's orders it seems likely that Izvestia will not be allowed by the Defense Ministry to run the full story as planned on the shooting down of KAL 007.

The Gorbachev Myth could not have been projected so successfully without the help of the West. The truth about Gorbachev has been there from the beginning. Of course, Gorbachev's public relations campaign exceeded all past glasnost and fake liberalization campaigns.

Gorbachev has consistently said that he is a Leninist and a Communist. On December 23, 1989, Gorbachev said **"I am a Communist. I shall remain a convinced one . . . for me it is a goal."** [27] Gorbachev said he has long looked to Lenin for answers. In a 1987 speech celebrating the 70th anniversary of the Bolshevik Revolution, Gorbachev said: **"We are moving toward a new world, the world of communism. We shall never turn off that road."** [28]

There are several accounts which documented and warned against such a false liberalization campaign by Moscow based on both inside information and on past history and practices of the Soviets.

Anatoliy Golitsyn, a KGB officer who defected to the West, published a book in 1984 entitled New Lies For Old. With uncanny accuracy, Golitsyn mentioned Soviet plans for a false liberalization in Eastern Europe and in the USSR carried out by a "Soviet Dubcek" (read Gorbachev) including such developments as the fall of the Berlin Wall, the emergence of multiparty regimes in Eastern European countries and even the withdrawal of some of the Communist states from the Warsaw Pact. [29]

In Deception, Jay Edward Epstein documents past Soviet glasnost campaigns and describes the success of Gorbachev's glasnost, "the Sixth Glasnost." Gorbachev's glasnost campaign has had unparalleled success in transforming the image of the Soviets from that of an enemy or adversary to that of a friend or even an ally (in the Persian Gulf and UN). Epstein writes that the image change resulted in large part from Soviet success in winning over the foreign media and academicians who became convinced that Soviet official organs were independent sources. So even though the Soviet press was still state owned or influenced (via permits and newsprint), the West bought into the great Soviet deception. And "at virtually no cost to Soviet power, the sixth Glasnost had provided the Soviet leadership with not only the tens of billions of dollars in credits . . .," but a much less threatening image. [30]

Why has the Bush Administration and State Department not read the situation right on Gorbachev, Deng Xiaoping and other Communist bosses? Why was there not one word of caution given before the administration jumped in bed with Gorbachev and Deng and Iliescu in Romania?

It cannot be due to a lack of knowledge, information, or intelligence reports. U.S. technological intelligence gathering is second to none. There are tens of millions of refugees, defectors, and immigrants from all Communist lands. Among these are dozens of former high ranking officials of the Soviet and East Bloc intelligence, military and foreign officials. They have given voluminous amounts of proof of the Soviet Communist record and practices, of tactics and strategy, and of the operating mentality of the leadership.

The proof was there regarding Gorbachev's practices, tactics, objectives, aims, and mentality, but the Bush Administration conveniently covers this up. [31] The record of Soviet, Chinese and East Bloc fake glasnost campaigns of the past have been exposed in print. Likely Soviet tactics including coalitions, puppet committees/ fronts and the Brest-Litovsk strategy of making tactical retreats via shocking "temporary" concessions have been written about at length. There have even been reports of the extent of Soviet active measures in influencing the U.S. political process and elections, which were covered up by the State Department. [32]

And the Deputy Director of the CIA in a briefing on the USSR & Gorbachev, gave clear warnings about the limits of glasnost, the continued Soviet weapons buildup, the mistake of our financing perestroika, and the "traditional" objectives of Gorbachev's foreign policy. [33]

In the midst of the great Gorbachev build-up in the Western press/media, there were reminders that Gorbachev was a disciple of former KGB chief Yuri Andropov who ordered the tanks to roll over Hungarians in 1956. And that Raisa Gorbachev wrote a doctoral thesis for the Moscow Order of the Red Banner for Labor State Pedagogical Institute on the need to brainwash peasants into giving up their religion and its "superstition." [34]

Yet none of this influenced the Bush Administration policy of buying into Gorbachev's fake program of democratization, liberalization and pacifism. The Soviet public relations campaign and propaganda were aided and abetted by the major media and U.S. officials feeding the media (often planting intact the intended Soviet disinformation).

Why did official Washington ignore the Soviet and Chinese Communist legacies of murder and human/cultural destruction? Why were high ranking defectors such as Soviet KGB Major Anatoliy Golitsyn, Polish Ambassador to Japan Dr. Zdislaw Rurarz, Romanian Securitate (KGB) chief Lt. General Ion Mihai Pacepa, and others ignored? Why, for crying out loud, won't George Bush meet with leading dissidents from the Communist countries? Perhaps he should call his friend Gerald Ford who admitted that his greatest regret as President was snubbing Soviet dissident Alexandr Solzhenitsyn.

Why were the accounts of influential immigrants/ defectors from the Baltics, Armenia, Georgia, Moldavia, and the Ukraine, ignored? Why were constant warnings about Gorbachev from

Andrei Sakharov and Elena Bonner, Gary Kasparov, Alexandr Solzhenitsyn, and even Eduard Shevardnadze ignored?

Why did Washington ignore the persistent — although conveniently downplayed in a major media busy creating the Good Gorbachev myth — accounts of continued Soviet acts of aggression and cruelty; continued Soviet aid to despotic communist regimes in Cuba and Afghanistan; and the continued Soviet massive military build-up and violations of military arms treaties?

If one could plausibly argue that FDR was too ill or too unaware of Soviet machinations (due in part to his right hand man Harry Hopkins serving as an agent), one could not make that case for Bush.

Bush was head of the CIA, chief of the US Mission in Beijing, Vice President and President (and head of a national security crisis management team), where he had full access to the highest level of intelligence information that exists. I was U.S. Ambassador to a sensitive post in Communist Romania and I saw such intelligence information. Bush could not have been unaware of or ignorant of the continuing ugly face of Gorbachev — his practices and objectives. He read the intelligence information. He saw the warnings from the Sakharovs and the Pacepas. So why would Bush look the other way?

I saw George Bush briefed and in fact briefed him myself on Communist atrocities on some occasions. Despite evidence of murderous policies and stolen technology and terrorist activity/drug running, he proceeded to reward the Romanian Communist regime. The fact is that his actions served to promote the one world government idea in alliance with the Communists — whose values are the opposite of ours.

His dealings with Communist tyrants have reflected the naive old convergence theory of leftists, that the American and Soviet systems are getting closer to each other. In fact, the convergence theorists actually believe it is a good thing for our two systems to become more alike!

President Bush's actions have also reflected a belief that Communist words can be accepted at face value. In view of all this, one can honestly ask why did and why does Bush continue such appeasement of and collaboration with tyrannical Communist regimes? Does he do it to protect the hundreds of big bankers, businessmen, corporate heads, and other Insider friends who have made big bucks from monopoly arrangements with Communist rulers? Does Bush do it because he and other Insiders actually believe in one world government and monopolistic control over the world economy and political affairs by those few who manipulate people through the control of wealth?

If Bush were a true fighter for freedom and democratic government, he could hardly assist the world's greatest slave empires and crushers of freedom. In fact why would Bush — if he understood anything about the real struggle for human dignity and freedom of the peoples in the USSR — consistently make the weakest response to acts of aggression and repression by the the Soviet Communists?

Even in the wake of the January 1991 massacres in the Baltics and Soviet duplicity in the Persian Gulf War from January to March 1991, Bush's White House focused on helping Gorbachev. Bush and his aides continue to talk of "arranging another superpower summit" and "giving Gorbachev a much needed domestic political boost." [35]

It is a sad commentary that Bush has chosen to help preserve Gorbachev and Soviet Communism at all costs rather than helping the long-suffering people of the USSR achieve their freedom.

CHAPTER 4

APPEASEMENT OF GORBACHEV IN THE BALTICS:

LITHUANIA'S PRESIDENT COMPARES BUSH'S POLICY TO "MUNICH"

DECEMBER 27, 1990:

GEORGE BUSH ON MIKHAIL GORBACHEV: "BUT THE MAIN THING IS THERE'S A DETERMINATION TO KEEP GOING DOWN THIS PATH OF REFORM, AND THAT'S VERY IMPORTANT"

. . . then 3 weeks later

JANUARY 11, 1991:

BUSH SAID GORBACHEV ASSURED HIM IN A TELEPHONE CALL THAT HE WANTED A PEACEFUL SOLUTION; VIKTOR NAKAS (SPOKESMAN FOR LITHUANIAN INFORMATION CENTER) SAID THE REAL PURPOSE OF THE CALL WAS "TO SEE HOW BUSH WOULD REACT ON THE LITHUANIAN ISSUE," AND THAT "BUSH GAVE A GREEN LIGHT TO DO ANYTHING HE [GORBACHEV] WANTS" ("Bush Remains Cautious on Baltic Events," The Washington Post, January 12, 1991)

JANUARY 11, 1991:

ALMOST SIMULTANEOUSLY SOVIET PARATROOPERS & TANKS MOVE ON THE LITHUANIAN CAPITAL, AND IN LESS THAN 48 HOURS (ON JANUARY 13TH), KILL 16 AND INJURE 600 UNARMED PEOPLE

still . . .

JANUARY 13, 1991:

BUSH STILL DOESN'T WANT TO BELIEVE THAT HIS MAN GORBACHEV WAS RESPONSIBLE: "BUSH SAID HE DID NOT KNOW WHETHER PRESIDENT MIKHAIL S. GORBACHEV HAD ORDERED THE SOVIET TANKS AND PARATROOPERS" (The News and Observer, January 14, 1991, p. 5A)

a week later . . .

JANUARY 20, 1991:

SOVIET TROOPS KILL 5 AND INJURE 12 IN LATVIA

JANUARY 22, 1991:

MARI-ANN RIKKEN, ESTONIAN NATIONAL COUNCIL VICE PRESIDENT USED THE WORD APPEASEMENT TO BUSH; SAID WASHINGTON "LOOKS THE OTHER WAY"; AND "BUSH TAKES AT FACE VALUE GORBACHEV'S CLAIMS THAT THE KILLINGS. . . WERE THE RESPONSIBILITY OF LOCAL ARMY OFFICERS."

FEBRUARY 3, 1991:

RED ARMY COLONEL SAYS: "GORBACHEV MUST HAVE BEEN INFORMED"

ITEM
- Soviet troops occupy & bully Lithuania in spring 1990
- Baltics plea for moral help from the West
- Soviet massacre in Lithuania & Latvia in January1991

U.S. REACTION: Business as usual
- Bush makes appeasing statements
- Lithuanian V.P. stands outside White House & gets second rate treatment
- Washington takes no strong steps against Soviets; assistance to Moscow continues; Baltic governments are not recognized & no help given

In a secret protocol of the Nazi-Soviet (Ribbentrop-Molotov) Pact of August 23, 1939, the independence of the Baltic states of Estonia, Latvia and Lithuania was snuffed out by Hitler and Stalin. In June 1940, the Soviets militarily occupied the three Baltic states and made them constituent republics of the USSR. The peoples of the Baltics states have remained under Soviet occupation against their will until now. The courageous peoples have never let the spirit of independence die and have served as symbols for all the world of determination, courage and indomitable spirit.

The legacy of the Soviet Communists in the Baltic states is one of invasion, occupation, repression, and murder. Persecution of religious and political opponents of the Soviet Communists (and their puppet governments) was severe. In Lithuania, the Communists singled out the Catholic church for extraordinary persecution and harassment. From 1945 to 1955 "4 bishops, 185 priests and 275,000 laymen were arrested, imprisoned or sent to Siberia from where most never returned," while "any form or method of religious instruction is forbidden. Even the parents are penalized for teaching or permitting their children to be taught religion. The practice of religion, even privately, is not tolerated." [1]

One Soviet secret police (NKVD) report of June 13, 1941 mentions "11,102 Estonians, 16,255 Latvians, and 21,114 Lithuanians — a total of 48,471 — who were herded into 871 freight cars and sent off to Siberia on that one day."[2] In all 35,000 Lithuanians were deported or killed during the first Soviet occupation in 1941 and 350,000 more were sent into the gulag system between 1944 and 1952.

In Latvia, the majority Lutheran church had one-third of its parishes closed and over three-fourths of its pastors either deported or exiled to the West. The overall decline in church life in Latvia and Estonia were reflected in the "reduced number of baptisms, confirmations, church weddings and funerals. These one-time national churches became local churches." [3]

The Soviets viewed the people of the Baltics as potential threats to Soviet rule, especially the religious believers. In December 1983, for example, Soviet authorities described an imprisoned Lithuanian Catholic priest as "an enemy — you and all believers are enemies of Soviet power."[4]

Since the beginning of the Soviet annexation of the Baltic states, the U.S. Government has not recognized the "illegal incorporation, by force of arms, of the States of Latvia, Lithuania, and Estonia by the Soviet Union." [5] The practical applications of the American policy have been State Department representation at the three missions (legations) of the independent Baltic states on their National Days, broadcasts to the Baltic peoples via Voice of America and Radio Free Europe, and statements by the U.S. Government on our "nonrecognition policy." Thus the U.S. has extended de jure recognition of the Baltic Republics. President Ronald Reagan made some of the strongest statements of solidarity with the Baltic peoples on the 61st anniversary of America's de jure recognition in July 1983:

> "Americans share the just aspirations of the Baltic nations for national independence. We cannot remain silent in the face of the continued refusal of the Government of the USSR to allow these people to be free. We uphold their right to determine their own national destiny . . . . For this reason, the Government of the United States has never recognized the forced incorporation of the Baltic states into the Soviet Union and will not do so in the future." [6]

In the spring of 1990, the Baltic nations took steps toward independence through the election of parliaments and declaration to "restore independence." Estonia declared independence on February 2nd. On February 24th, Lithuania elected representatives to parliament in a free and democratic election for the first time since the Communist takeover. The Sajudis independence movement won 90% of the seats in parliament, and on March 11th, the parliament declared that Lithuania was once again an independent state. On May 4th, the newly elected Latvian parliament voted to declare the restoration of independence.

After the Lithuanians made the independence declaration, the borders were sealed, MIG's flew overhead, foreign journalists were kicked out, military deserters and others were beaten by Soviet troops, Soviet media disinformation was disseminated, and tanks rumbled through the streets of Lithuania's capital, Vilnius. Additionally, Gorbachev turned off gas and fuel supplies and slapped an economic blockade on Lithuania. Gorbachev said he would not use force in Lithuania. That was a lie.

Gorbachev thus strangled Lithuania's attempts at independence in March and April 1990. It was then clear that Gorbachev had no intention of allowing independence for the Balltic republics or other states in the Soviet Union. Gorbachev had tricked the West into believing that he would grant independence to the Baltics over a period of time if only they followed the prescribed procedures. As Gorbachev put it on May 14, 1990, the Baltics must follow a new secession law, which requires approval by residents in a referendum, a waiting period of five years and final approval by the Soviet leadership. [7] In other words, not really, not now, not ever.

While running for President, Bush had promised to support Lithuania's efforts for freedom.

Just before his 1988 election, **Bush wrote an American Lithuanian spokesman, Povilas Janciauskas, promising that the U.S.:**

> **"WILL NEVER CONDONE THE FORCED OCCUPATION OF LITHUANIA BY THE SOVIET UNION. TO DO SO WOULD BE TO TURN OUR BACKS ON OUR VALUES AND HERITAGE. AS A NATION BORN OUT OF A STRUGGLE AGAINST TYRANNY, AMERICANS SHOULD NEVER APOLOGIZE FOR HELPING OTHERS WIN THEIR FREEDOM, AND I NEVER WILL. AND SO, AS WE ENTER THE FINAL STRETCH OF THE CAMPAIGN, I WOULD RESPECTFULLY REQUEST THAT YOU SUPPORT MY CANDIDACY."** [8]

But after becoming President, Bush completely abandoned the Lithuanians and other Baltic peoples. Bush chose to ignore the declarations of independence by the Baltic republics even though U.S. policy since the 1940's had been to not recognize the forced incorporation into the Soviet Union (recognition of de jure independence). [9]

Bush and his administration made statement after statement indicating that they were turning their backs on Lithuania's freedom drive in spite of Bush's campaign promise.

AP/WIDE WORLD PHOTOS

Bush welcomes Gorbachev to the Oval Office just weeks after the Soviets bully Lithuania. May 31, 1990

On April 1, 1990, Bush said: **"I'd say let them sort it out," because "they're on the right track."** [10]

During the week of April 16th, Bush said: **"There's a great desire to know . . . What the President of the US [can] do to force change upon somebody— and it's not that clear."** [11] When Bush told Baltic-Americans: **"people think I'm a coldblooded elitist, but I'm not,"** people were right! [12]

On the first of May, when Lithuanian Prime Minister Kazimiera Prunskiene arrived at the White House "Much to the annoyance of 'unnamed top presidential advisers;" " . . . she had to get out of her car, show a Soviet (not a Lithuanian) passport, and wait in line with the tourists for 10 minutes before being allowed to walk up the path to the White House entrance.'" [13] The same White

House that rolled out the carpet for Nelson Mandela (man of violence, African National Congress leader and unrepentant Marxist revolutionary) received her in "a mean-spirited and insulting manner. She was stopped at the White House gate by security guards, her purse was searched . . ., and "went out of its way to humiliate Prime Minister Prunskiene." [14]

Also on the first of May, Bush said **"I'm concerned that we not inadvertently do something that compels the Soviet Union to take action that would set back the whole case of freedom around the world."** [15] George Will said "something we might say or do might "compel" a Soviet attack on freedom? That is the mentality of an apologist." [16]

On the first of May, a Bush aide made the despicable wisecrack: **"We're not going to cancel the summit just because Lithuanian housewives can't heat their coffee on Saturday morning."** [17]

To top it all off, in late April a White House aide said that even if Gorbachev cracked down on Lithuania "we're talking somewhere above 'deeply concerned' but well below canceling the summit . . . **we're talking relatively small potatoes."** [18]

The White House reaction to Lithuania's declaration of independence in the spring of 1990 recalls Secretary of State John Foster Dulles's reaction to the Hungarian uprising in 1956: the U.S. is not interested in intervening in the internal affairs of the Soviet Bloc. The Lithuanian independence action was an embarassment to the Bush Administration.

Yet the Lithuanians never asked for our money or even our blood, but only our moral support through a declaration of recognition of the overwhelmingly elected government of Lithuania. We should never be neutral in the defense of freedom. Lithuanian prisoner of conscience (over 21 years in Soviet prisons) Father Alfonsas Svarinskas perceptively said that "people in the United States are losing their faith . . . in God and putting their faith in Gorbachev. In Lithuania most people believe in God, and they don't believe in Gorbachev. No one believes in Gorbachev in Lithuania, unless they are psychologically sick." [19] Lithuanian Bishop Antanas Vaicius in a letter of April 25, 1990, to Bush said: "The Lithuanian people do not expect any military assistance from the United States nor a military confrontation between the two super-powers. We ask for moral and political support from the United States."[20]

A Lithuanian Supreme Council member, Valdas Katkus, warned that: "if the West is worried about offending Gorbachev or hurting him . . . then we are little more than hostages to Moscow."[21] As George Will mockingly put it: "Bush's policy is to do whatever is necessary to 'save' Gorbachev. Even acquiesce in his strangulation of Lithuania. Otherwise Gorbachev might fail and be followed by a bad man — the sort who would strangle Lithuania."![22] Unfortunately the White House was worried about upsetting Gorbachev more than about concern for freedom of the Baltic states. The White House statements in the wake of Soviet bullying of Lithuania in the spring of 1990 gave a clear green light for Gorbachev to more harshly crackdown.

The cynicism of the Soviets and their unreliability were made clear by their economic and financial moves before the tanks rolled into Lithuania and Latvia. The Soviets went on a spending binge in the U.S. with American credits, buying grain from Soviet trade partners Archer Daniels Midland Company and Continental Grain Company just before they rolled tanks over Lithuanians and Latvians. Gorbachev used up $1 billion in Commodity Credit Corporation (CCC) credits and some $10 billion in new government loans and cheap credits from Western banks and governments. [23]

Gorbachev had ensured that the West would be so economically tied to the Soviets that any retreat of capital investment would be unlikely. By the time of his bloody crackdown in the Baltics, Gorbachev had helped attract some 3,000 joint ventures from the West including the following big deals: American Trade Consortium (Chevron, Johnson & Johnson, RJR Nabisco, Eastman Kodak, and Archer Daniels Midland) for $10 billion; Combustion Engineering for $2.2 billion; and American Medical Consortium (Pitzer, Hewlett-Packard, and Colgate-Palmolive) for $2 billion. [24] Thus Gorbachev had snookered the West into financially and economically buying into perestroika before he blatantly showed his true colors.

On January 13, 1991, with the West conveniently preoccupied with its attack on Iraqi forces to liberate Kuwait (to begin in three days), Soviet tanks and troops fired on unarmed civilians in Vilnius, Lithuania, killing 16 (including women and children) and wounding over 600 more. Eduardas Potashinskas, a worker at Lithuanian TV, described it saying: "they are driving their tanks right at the people," and "they are beating people. They are beating women!" [25] Another eyewitness, Teresa Kosloskine, saw the Soviet tanks "without notice, they lurched forward, knocked people down, and ran over some of those lying prone," including two boys. [26]

Exactly a week later, on January 20, 1991, the Lithuanian massacre was followed by Soviet tanks and shock troops (black beret commandos) shooting at Latvians, killing four and wounding a dozen more. Moscow even argued that the military was acting to restore power (Moscow's rule) at the behest of newly created National Salvation Committees (or Fronts) set up by the local Communist parties. The Lithuanian and Latvian National Salvation Committees were thus set up by Gorbachev based on the model used by Gorbachev's old friend Romanian President Ion Iliescu. [27]

Bush's reaction to the massacres in Lithuania and Latvia was one of appeasement. Bush still did not want to believe that his man Gorbachev was responsible for the murders, saying **"he [Bush] did not know whether President Mikhail S. Gorbachev had ordered the Soviet tanks and paratroopers."** [28]

But even a Red Army Colonel indicated that Gorbachev was lying about not giving the order for the massacres. Red Army Colonel Viktor Alksnis said what everyone in the USSR knew: "Gorbachev must have been informed," because "any movement of armed troops in the Soviet Union can occur only if the President gives an order or is informed." [29]

Bush gave a green light in his telephone conversations and other signals for Gorbachev to attack in the Baltics. On the first day of the Soviet paratroopers actions in Vilnius, January 11th, Bush reported that in a telephone conversation "Gorbachev knows my position (on Lithuania)." [30] Bush "talked on the phone to his friend Gorbachev" mildly hinting that "Soviet-American relations <u>might</u> be affected if there were any intensification of repression. On January 13, he read a press statement in which he . . . urged Soviet leaders to refrain from 'further acts that might lead to more violence and loss of life.'"[31] The message was clear to Gorbachev since the repression was already in place from his point of view.

Bush let Moscow know that preservation of the new U.S.-Soviet relationship was more important than the lives of brave Lithuanians and Latvians who stood for freedom and independence from Soviet Communism. On January 13th, Bush stated that

> **"for several years now, the Soviet Union has been on a course of democratic and peaceful change, and we've supported that effort, and stated repeatedly how much we admire the Soviet leaders who chose that path. Indeed, change in the Soviet Union has helped to create a basis for unprecedented cooperation and partnership between the United States and the Soviet Union."**[32]

Jack Mendelsohn of the Arms Control Association explained that "It's rather coldblooded, but at some point the question becomes whether 50 Balts are as important to the U.S. national interest as 50,000 Soviet nuclear warheads. I think no." [33]

And National Security Adviser Brent Scowcroft told Baltic leaders "there's an absolute necessity to 'save' Gorbachev for America's sake — to prevent the Soviet Union from spinning off into anarchy."[34] That's like giving Gorbachev carte blanche to do whatever he wants.

It is no wonder that Baltic leaders have expressed outrage at Bush's lack of support. Lithuania's President Vytautus Landsbergis compared Bush's policy with that of the West at **Munich**. Viktor Nakas, spokesman for a Lithuanian Information Center in the U.S. said that by "giving only a 'pro-forma protest' to Gorbachev, **Bush was giving the Soviet leader 'a green light to do anything he wants.'"** [35]

Tunne Kelam, Chairman of the Congress of Estonia, and Mari-Ann Rikken, Vice President of the Estonian-American National

Council, said that Bush has "drawn a line in the sand in the Middle East but **is putting his head in the sand in Europe**," and that "we are facing a crucial test not only for the survival of the Baltic nations but also for the principles of American foreign policy. Lasting world peace and stability cannot be achieved by applying principles of justice and law unequally." [36]

Baltic leaders, distressed about Bush's appeasement policy, also pointed out that the implications of Gorbachev's actions (and Bush's weak response) for the future. Lithuanian Vice President Bronius Kuzmickas in late January asked the U.S. to look to the future and realize the "Baltics are the crucial test. If democratization is stopped in the Baltic states, it will be in the Soviet Union as well."[37]

Latvia's Foreign Minister Jainis Jurkans warned that "if [Western governments] do not succeed in bringing a clear message, I think the Soviets will get back to Eastern Europe like before." [38] Latvia's Vice President Dainis Ivans declared that "economic assistance to the central Soviet government must be stopped," and that official recognition be extended to the democratically elected Baltic governments. [39] Ivans continued to say that "without forceful and consistent pressure by the United States on the Gorbachev government, democratization will be destroyed in the Baltic states, Russia and beyond." [40]

Even some in Congress have belatedly come to realize that U.S. aid to the Soviet central government in Moscow only serves to preserve the Communist system and snuff out freedom movements in the Soviet republics.

Senator Bob Dole is the Republican leader in the Senate in charge of pushing Bush's programs through Congress and one who has carried water for the White House in the past to Moscow and Bucharest. But even he acknowledged in February 1991 that the Bush policy of sending food and aid to the central Soviet government to prop up Gorbachev is wrong. Dole says:

> "I think as far as food and money, we ought to be dealing with the republics. We ought to be helping the Baltic states — Armenia, other republics in the Soviet Union — rather than the central government, because they've been using

> our food to intimidate the republics to sign the union treaty or do certain things." [41]

And Senator Alfonse D'Amato expressed the outrage many Americans feel when they see Western aid going to a Soviet Government that is massacring people in the Baltics:

> "West Germany is going to give the Soviets multiple billions in aid. Maybe they will help the Russians build some new highways so their tanks will have a smoother ride when they drive into the Baltics." [42]

Even some leftist Democrats are speaking out against Mikhail Gorbachev's brutal repression of the Baltics. Liberal Congresswoman Patricia Schroeder (D-Colorado) said:

> "I must say, too, that I think Gorbachev should either surrender his Peace Prize or that the Nobel Peace Committee should reclaim it, that President Bush should take back our aid and that we should also ask the Saudis and others to take back their aid if this continues." [43]

Yet, George Bush continues to gush praise for Mikhail Gorbachev. It is incredible that a Republican President claiming to be a conservative can find himself to the left of leftist Democrats on the issue of confronting Communist aggression. How many Lithuanian and Latvian citizens does Mikhail Gorbachev have to kill before George Bush wakes up and smells the coffee?

Or as one reader of US News and World Report put it: When will Bush set "the deadline for Mikhail Gorbachev to withdraw from Lithuania or else face the military consequences?" [44]

Two small countries even had the guts to stick their necks out and do what was morally right. Tiny NATO ally Iceland and Soviet neighbor Czechoslovakia announced in February 1991 their intention to recognize the government of Lithuania. [45]

Tiny Iceland became a giant by granting formal diplomatic recognition to Lithuania. John Budris, until recently a correspondent for Radio Vilnius World Service, explained the special courage of Iceland in a New York Times letter "Iceland Puts the West to Shame on Baltics." Budris pointed out that Iceland's Foreign Minister Jon Baldvin Hannibalsson returned from a trip in January to Vilnius "where along with a million mourners, he attended the funeral of the 15 [16] slaughtered by Soviet tanks and machine guns in the siege of the broadcast center." [46]

Hannibalsson understood that the appeasement began a year earlier in March 1990 when the Soviets bullied Lithuania. That was the time for the West to embrace Baltic independence. But "the West chose instead to appease the Soviets and cast the Baltic independence drives as the stick in the eye of Mr. Gorbachev's perestroika." [47] That is why Iceland decided to do something to rectify past mistakes of the West.

The Czechoslovaks who suffered under the 1968 Soviet invasion (and still have Soviet occupying troops and a common border with the USSR) actually risked more by showing their support of the Lithuanians than George Bush as the leader of the Free World was willing to do.

The Bush Administration record toward Soviet actions against the Baltics states has been one of appeasement. During the most critical moment in the 50 years since they were overrun by the Soviet Union, the peoples of the Baltics have been sold out by the Bush Administration.

Maintenance of the New World Order relationship of Bush and Gorbachev has assumed a higher priority than advancing the freedom of the people of the Baltics. First in 1990 and again in 1991 Bush signalled to the valiant peoples of the Baltics not to expect American help — even morally and symbolically. And at the same time he whetted the appetite of the latest Soviet tyrant.

The Bush Foreign Policy Establishment has not wanted Americans to see the real side of Gorbachev which has been there all along — the Gorbachev of chemical weapons and gas, troops and tanks, conventional weapons and live bullets used against civilians at least five times before Lithuania and Latvia: in Kazakhstan in December 1986; Tbilisi, Georgia, April 8, 1989; Parkent, Uzbekistan, June 1989 (and again March 1990); Azerbaijan,

January 20, 1990; and Dushanbe, Tajikistan, February 11-14, 1990. [48]

Unfortunately, George Bush and Company believe in the good face of Gorbachev, the sell job of glasnost, perestroika, and Gorbachev the peaceful reformer. The final words of Lithuanian President Landsbergis to the visiting Executive Director of the US Helsinki Watch Committee, Jeri Laber, were: "Push Bush." [49]

But the Soviet action in the Baltics should have called into question all of the premises on which Bush's foreign and defense policies were operating. If the Soviets are not peaceful and Soviet conduct has not fundamentally changed, then why did Bush begin the process of disarmament and shoveling U.S. taxpayer dollars to the Soviet Communists? [50]

POLICY RECOMMENDATIONS:

- As long as Soviet troops occupy the Baltic states to prevent independence and continue to kill innocent people, there must be no U.S. MFN, no trade credits, no relaxed controls on technology transfer, no aid or financing.
- The U.S. should formally recognize the Baltic states and send ambassadors to the countries.
- The U.S. should trade directly with the Baltic governments.
- The U.S. should strongly condemn the Soviet massacre in Lithuania & Latvia and take concrete steps to show that such actions adversely affect the US-USSR relations; and the U.S. should broadcast via its radio stations to the whole world that such actions by Moscow violate the norms of civilized behavior and will not be tolerated.

George Bush was the highest ranking official to meet with Ceausescu during the 1980's. September, 1983

CHAPTER 5

APPEASEMENT OF NICOLAE CEAUSESCU IN ROMANIA: BUSH SUPPORTS U.S. AID TO COMMUNISTS

ITEM: NICOLAE CEAUSESCU'S REIGN OF TERROR, 1965-1989

- thousands of religious and political dissidents killed
- over one million non-criminals arrested and jailed
- over one hundred thousand orphans placed in inhuman conditions
- hundreds of churches destroyed (including 24 in Bucharest)
- hundreds of historical villages demolished
- tens of thousands of historic dwellings & monuments destroyed
- hundreds of thousands working for the dreaded Securitate
- over ten thousand spies infiltrated the U.S. and West
- Orwellian policies such as the scientific diet, the typewriter decree, 5 child per woman requirement

BUSH'S REACTION: BUSINESS AS USUAL

- praise and support for Ceausescu by Bush, Nixon and others
- Bush travels to Romania and lends Ceausescu even more legitimacy
- MFN and other economic assistance (as well as a higher level of technology) continued from 1985 to 1988

In December 1989 the whole world caught a glimpse [on television following Ceausescu's demise] of the horrors that had been taking place in Romania under totalitarian Communists. But other than the plight of the orphans, AID's victims, Securitate (secret police) crimes, and the extravagant Ceausescu family life styles, few details have emerged regarding the people killed and churches destroyed under Ceausescu.

The sad thing is that George Bush, Lawrence Eagleburger and the foreign policy establishment knew about the horrors of Ceausescu years before Ceausescu's downfall. I know. I saw many of the reports detailing Ceausescu's crimes. But the foreign policy establishment didn't lift a finger to stop it. In fact, George Bush and the foreign policy establishment actually sent aid to prop up Ceausescu's reign of terror.

George Bush was the highest Reagan Administration official to travel to Romania, the highest Reagan Administration official to meet with Ceausescu, and the highest Reagan Administration official to take an active role in U.S. policy towards Romania.

And George Bush's support of Ceausescu and U.S. aid to Ceausescu never wavered.

As you read the following details about Ceausescu's murderous regime, think about this: *What does it say about a man (George Bush) who would support such a murderous regime? And what does it say about George Bush's judgement and values when he names as his number two man at the State Department a man (Eagleburger) who consistently overlooked the crimes of the Ceausescu regime?*

By piecing together scores of reports from Amnesty International, Helsinki Watch, Keston News Service, U.S. Senate and House Foreign Relations and Trade Committee hearings on MFN for Romania, prominent defectors, and religious figures, one can get a better overall picture of the magnitude of the crimes carried out by Ceausescu's regime.

There were thousands of religious and political dissidents killed by the Ceausescu regime and hundreds of thousands more arrested and jailed for opposition to the state and/or Ceausescu. Some authoritative accounts put the figure of those classified as enemies of the state and imprisoned in labor camps as exceeding one million. [1] Romanian Orthodox Church priest Father Gheorghe Calciu-Dumitreasa who spent 21 years in prison (under Ceausescu) told me on February 18, 1991, that over 50,000 opponents of the regime were arrested in addition to the thousands of miners for their demonstrations against poor working conditions in the Jiu Valley coal mines in 1978 alone. Many families were dislocated as a result of the miner's strike and establishment of a short-lived free trade union. [2]

The story of the Romanian orphans and AIDS victims has been widely publicized since the December 1989 upheaval in Romania. In fact since ABC-TV broadcast on 20/20 the horrible plight of the abandoned children crowded into the state orphanages, a senior editor of 20/20 said the result was "the greatest outpouring of humanitarian response ever received by a network." [3] The Romanian emigre newspaper Lumea Libera has reported that the total number of orphans in Romania exceeds 100,000, while Newsweek reported that perhaps as many as 130,000 orphans have been left in the 300 or so institutions unfit for human habitation.[4]

Another anti-religious and anti-Western Civilization policy of Ceausescu's was the destruction of irreplaceble churches, villages, historical monuments, and dwellings. The thousands of churches destroyed by Ceausescu included at least 24 historic ones in Bucharest and one of the most notable monastery complexes in the country (Vacaresti). Other churches demolished include the Enei Church in 1977, the Cotroceni Church in 1984, the St. Nicolae Sirbi Church in 1985, and a Seventh Day Adventist church, a Sephardic Synagogue and St. Nicolae-Jitnita all in 1986. [5] Outside Bucharest, Adventist, Baptist, Brethren, Calvinist, Catholic, Lutheran, Pentecostal, Orthodox churches and others were destroyed on a regular basis. [6]

Ceausescu began a "systematization" process of village demolition throughout the country. The objective was to destroy the traditional monuments and churches and over 7,000 villages which tied the people to their centuries-old traditions and civilization. The historic villages were to be replaced by agro-industrial centers and apartment blocks where all individuals could be even more closely observed and controlled by the government. Before Ceausescu's demise, over 29 towns were completely destroyed, 38 towns were largely demolished, and many others were partially destroyed. Massive destruction of Romania's capital and largest city Bucharest took place beginning in 1984 with the demolition of hundreds of historic buildings. [7] Additionally, tens of thousands of old dwellings and public monuments were razed nationwide. [8]

The damage to Romania's cultural and religious heritage is incalculable. As Dinu Giurescu puts it: "Romania will stand forever as the most vivid example of how wholesale demolition of the urban and rural fabric can be perpetrated to subvert the identity of a nation. Beneath the surface lay the theoretical scheme aimed at controlling the private and public lives of the populace." [9]

The number of people working for Ceausescu's Securitate numbered in the hundreds of thousands, with additional millions occasionally reporting on others inside the country. The Romanian espionage service was so large and active that over 10,000 agents worked in the U.S. and West to control the exile community, "to destroy or neutralize anti-communist organizations, to recruit agents, and to improve Ceausescu's image in the West." [10] Former Romanian Securitate chief Ion Mihai Pacepa has documented their widespread and effective operations in the West including those involving U.S. Presidents and Ambassadors. [11] Other high ranking Securitate defectors such as Liviu Turcu and high ranking Foreign Ministry defectors such as Mircea Raceanu have confirmed many such operations.

Other bizarre policies of Ceausescu included a scientific diet counseling people to not eat meat (there was little meat available); a typewriter decree requiring the registration of all printing machines (copiers, typewriters, etc.); and the requirement that each woman during child-bearing years between 15 and 45 should have more than four children or face penalties. Women were regularly checked (by government doctors) for pregnancy and required to carry out the pregnancy.

In addition to the deaths, jailings, and overall repressive policies, the mental, psychological and spiritual damage to the remaining population has been the most long lasting legacy of destruction. One account notes that the worst legacy of the Ceausescu period is neither the devastated economy nor the pervasive poverty of the country, but rather the way four and one half decades of Communist rule has warped the human psyche. As

Giurescu described it: "after 45 years of Communist rule, the country has been psychologically crippled and physically lowered to sub-minimal standards. People fear each other. They are suspicious of minorities, of foreigners, and even of returning Romanian emigrants. Envy and hostility prevail over civic spirit; profiteering and idleness over steady work . . . ." [12]

Many dissidents, high-ranking defectors, and human rights organizations and religious groups reported many of the horrors of Ceausescu's reign of terror. From 1981 to 1985 I sent cables and letters to Washington detailing many of Ceausescu's murderous policies. Additionally in the course of one year and a half I sent dozens of letters to key figures questioning MFN and technology transfer to Bucharest and mentioning Ceausescu's madness. From September 1982 to May 1984, letters were sent to Assistant Secretary of State Elliott Abrams, Deputy Defense Secretary Frank Carlucci, National Security Adviser William Clark, NSC Officer Paula Dobriansky, NSC Officer Dr. Roy Godson, Senator Jesse Helms, Secretary of State George Shultz, Ambassador Faith Ryan Whittlesey, and many others. So there is no question of Washington not knowing what was happening in Romania under Ceausescu. At the same time the U.S. was continuing to grant MFN and send other assistance.

The Bush reaction was to ignore these reports and take actions which supported the Ceausescu dictatorship.

In spite of my reluctance and that of some other officers in the American Embassy, Bucharest, Bush traveled to Romania and helped give legitimacy to Ceausescu. In Bucharest, Bush disregarded my advice and praised Ceausescu. He also unwisely let Ceausescu manipulate the visit, changing the pre-arranged schedule. Ceausescu used the visit and Bush's favorable comments to the fullest, with the state media showing Bush's support for and homage to Ceausescu. Romanian television, radio, and newspapers were totally dominated by Bush's meetings with Ceausescu. (NOTE PHOTOS AND MEDIA REPORTS)

In addition to his visit to Romania, Bush received several high ranking Romanian Communist officials such as Foreign Minister Stefan Andrei in his office in Washington. MFN and other economic

BUSH & EAGLEBURGER: Prime architects of pro-Ceausescu policy are now supporting Communist National Salvation Front in Romania.

Vice President Bush meeting with Ceausescu in 1983.

Eagleburger with Ceausescu. 1983

Proletari din toate țările, uniți-vă!

România liberă

COTIDIANUL CONSILIULUI NAȚIONAL AL FRONTULUI DEMOCRAȚIEI ȘI UNITĂȚII SOCIALISTE

Anul XLI Nr. 12093 | Luni 19 septembrie 1983 | 6 pagini 30 bani

În cursul zilei de ieri

PREȘEDINTELE NICOLAE CEAUȘESCU

a primit pe vicepreședintele Statelor Unite ale Americii, George Bush

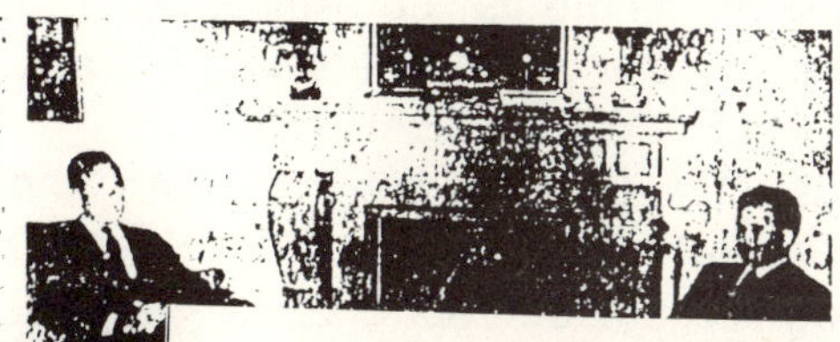

PROLETARI DIN TOATE ȚĂRILE, UNIȚI-VĂ!

Scînteia

ORGAN AL COMITETULUI CENTRAL AL PARTIDULUI COMUNIST ROMÂN

Anul LIII Nr. 12775 | Marți 20 septembrie 1983 | 6 PAGINI – 50 BANI

PREȘEDINTELE NICOLAE CEAUȘESCU

a primit pe vicepreședintele Statelor Unite ale Americii, George Bush

(such as CCC credits) assistance for Ceausescu continued throughout the Reagan-Bush Administration until Ceausescu renounced it in 1988.

Sadly, playing the game was more important to Washington than standing in solidarity with those in Romania seeking freedom and democratic government. The game of selling out the concerns of those seeking freedom from Communism in Romania began at Yalta. The policy of Washington collaborating with the Romanian Communists and sending assistance to Bucharest which helped solidify Communist power began in earnest with Nixon and Kissinger and their "differentiation policy." Nixon's many visits to Romania and praise for Ceausescu constitute an incredible betrayal of our principles. During my tenure as U.S. Ambassador to Romania, Nixon visited Ceausescu and sent letters or greetings and praise. (NOTE THE BUSH LETTER TO CEAUSESCU)

On August 11, 1983, I met with President Ronald Reagan and Vice President George Bush in the White House Oval Office. During the meeting I recounted the horrors of Ceausescu's tyrannical regime and the fact that I was warned to back off from sending cables to Washington describing such horrors (and recommending withdrawing U.S. aid for the Romanian Communists unless human rights violations ceased and free emigration was practiced). I told the President that then Under-Secretary of State Lawrence Eagleburger sent cables warning me not to rock the boat of cozy U.S.-Romanian relations by further emphasizing Ceausescu's murderous policies. President Reagan seemed surprised to hear this unhappy information, but at least expressed some sympathy with my position and encouragement for me to continue reporting things as I saw them.

By contrast George Bush showed no sympathy for the plight of Romanian religious believers who were severely persecuted when not killed or for the political dissidents who were repressed and herded into a vast gulag of slave labor camps of Ceausescu. Bush's concern instead was that I had dared to circumvent normal channels (i.e. the Secretary of State) to take the message directly to the President of a failed US policy rewarding one of the world's great monsters.

BUSH'S PERSONAL LETTER TO ROMANIAN DICTATOR NICOLAE CEAUSESCU.

9-21-83
enroute to USA

Dear Mr. President,

My sincere thanks to you and Mrs. Ceausescu for our long chat and for that special family dinner. I learned a great deal.

Our trip was far too brief but I saw enough to heighten my respect for the Romanian people and to hope that our relations continue to improve. My sincere thanks for the visit and for the lovely Rug you gave us too. Respectfully

Geo. Bush

Bush meets with a Communist dictator and then claims he "learned a great deal," when in reality he learned nothing of the tragic situation in Romania.

Apparently it had not bothered Bush that Ceausescu was terrorizing his country and still getting U.S. Most Favored Nation trade status assistance, or that I was being pressured by State Department officials to keep the Ceausescu-Washington relationship intact. After all, Bush — the ultimate insider — was confident that his foreign policy "genius" friends in the career bureaucracy of the State Department were doing the diplomatic thing and carrying out a proper status quo policy.

Thus George Bush, alone of those in my meeting with President Reagan, left the session without saying an encouraging word for me. Instead Bush asked incredulously "can things be that bad over at the State Department?" in terms of our policy vis-a-vis Eastern Europe in general and Romania in particular.

Following the meeting Bush rushed down the hall to call his insider friend Secretary of State George Shultz. Shultz then telephoned me in North Carolina, where I had just flown for a few days following Washington consultations. I was summoned to Shultz's office at the State Department. I was dressed down by Shultz for "criticizing him or his department before the President." Interestingly, like Reagan and the others, Shultz indicated no specific knowledge of developments in Romania and Eastern Europe, simply stating that he thought Larry (Eagleburger) was taking care of things in that part of the world. Unfortunately, Larry was! He was aiding Ceausescu's Communist regime.

I also had other meetings with George Bush when high level Romanian officials visited Washington, and when he visited Ceausescu in Romania. In a Washington meeting with Romanian Foreign Minister Stefan Andrei, Bush appeared to echo the briefings he got from State and NSC officials to appease Ceausescu (on May 17, 1983). Bush told Andrei he wanted to visit Romania and talk with Ceausescu, exactly what the Romanian Communists wanted to hear and what they had been pushing for — for propaganda and economic-financial purposes. Bush in his friendly meeting with the slippery Andrei said nothing tough and failed to demand improvement in Romania's horrible human rights records, emigration policy, or general repressiveness [13]

In several meetings between George Bush and high Romanian officials in Washington and Bucharest, Bush showed no concern for the massive human rights violations carried out by the terrible Ceausescu regime.

Bush was not concerned enough about human rights to speak out or even mention the state sponsored murder of a dissident Roman Catholic priest, or the murders of Baptist, Pentecostal and other pastors and priests in Romania. Hundreds of churches were bulldozed by the Ceausescu regime. Religious activities in general were severely restricted, and religious activists were strongly persecuted when not killed at the orders of the communist government. Reports of such religious and human rights violations were regularly sent to the State Department, the NSC, and White House, reaching Vice President George Bush. I personally helped brief Bush on his trip to see Ceausescu in Romania in the fall of 1983. He was asked to put down a marker for human rights and for the values and beliefs that America has long represented. Unfortunately not a finger was lifted by Bush.

Of course this same Bush failed to demonstrate concern for the plight of the persecuted in Communist China in the wake of Tiananmen Square, or for those repressed in the Baltics states, Armenia, Georgia and elsewhere in the Soviet Union.

Always the greater global interests of maintaining close ties with Communist bosses (known by and considered friends by Bush) took precedence for Bush over the concerns of the pro-freedom, democratic forces struggling for liberation. Always Bush relied on the faulty advice of careerists at the State Department who consistently counseled maintaining the status quo with Communist regimes (usually meaning favored treatment and assistance from the U.S. Government).

There is a disturbing sidelight to Bush's non-concern for human rights abuses conducted by Communist regimes such as those in Romania, China, and the USSR. In at least two meetings I attended between Bush and Romania's Foreign Minister Stefan Andrei, Bush called attention to the consular case (immigration) of one Andrei Coler. Where a personal friend or political connection

WHITE HOUSE PHOTO

George Bush meets with Ceausescu's Foreign Minister in the Vice-President's Office. May 16, 1983

was involved, Bush had an interest in getting a favorable resolution to a case.

The only case Bush mentioned in dealings with Ceausescu's Government was that of Andrei Coler, who was related by marriage to former Pennsylvania Governor Milton J. Shapp's son and who desired immigration to the U.S. from Romania. Shapp's son

Richard, married a Romanian of Jewish origin (Luminita Coler) whose brother and family had applied for emigration from Romania with little success. Andrei Coler's wife was Elena Rautu Coler, the daughter of Leonte Rautu (a ranking member of Ceausescu's Communist Politburo). Upon the request of Shapp, Bush became interested in the Andrei Coler family (wife Elena and daughter Alexandra) case. Because of the Vice President's interest, State Department officials worked to resolve the case. It is rather sad that the only known Romanian case in which Bush took an interest involved the family of one of Romania's most despised Communists Leonte Rautu. Rautu was "one of the oldest members of the Romanian Communist Party," who had survived every post-revolutionary change of government and held a ranking position on the Politburo. [14]

Equally troubling was the information that Andrei Coler's father—Colonel Stefan Coler—was the hated guard at Ceausescu's worst prison camp, where political and religious dissidents were severely beaten. Stefan Coler has been described as one who carried out the beatings with special relish. In his book, Journey to Freedom Nicholas Dima described his concern in these words: "Stefan Coler, the former Secret Police informer and the former commandant of Aiud, one of the most dreaded prisons in Communist Romania, was coming to the United States as an innocent man." [15]

I had referred to the Andrei Coler case in my book Pinstripes and Reds, detailing my experiences as U.S. Ambassador to Communist Romania between 1981 and 1985. Apparently because of the references made to Coler in my book, it became a concern for the Bush Presidential campaign committee. During Bush's campaign for President in 1988, I was contacted by a White House official regarding Coler. I was asked if I planned to do anything with the information I had on Andrei Coler during the campaign. Undoubtedly the Bush people were worried about any adverse publicity and were working to preempt any such action by preparing a "cover" story. To me such White House attention indicated that there was a problem with the Coler case. Andrei Coler — dubious recipient of Bush's attention and concern — appeared to be the only Romanian immigration case of interest to Bush.

Of all the deserving families in Romania, Bush went to bat for a family which included one of the highest ranking Communist colleagues of Ceausescu and one who tortured opponents of the Communist regime! Human rights and humanitarian concerns did not enter into Bush's policy formulations vis-a-vis Communists in Eastern Europe, the USSR or China.

BUSH AS PRESIDENT—CONTINUES SUPPORT OF CEAUSESCU AND HIS COMMUNIST SUCCESSOR, ION ILIESCU

ITEM: THE POST-CEAUSESCU COMMUNIST REGIME OF ION ILIESCU AND THE NATIONAL SALVATION FRONT (NSF)

- a KGB-GRU directed coup replaces Ceausescu with Gorbachev protege; most of the same Communist and Securitate officials stay in place
- unfair and unfree elections take place giving Communists victory
- opposition parties and publications suppressed by the NSF
- Securitate continues to operate much as before — intimidating people
- NSF-Iliescu-directed "miners" beat up anti-Communist demonstrators and trash offices of opposition parties
- economy dramatically worsens during the winter of 1990-91 with prices up almost three times while wages remain the same except for the "miners"

BUSH'S REACTION: BUSINESS AS USUAL

- Bush sends a big financial contributor as U.S. Ambassador who supports the Communist NSF
- Secretary of State Baker encourages Soviet troops to go into Romania
- Bush sends an election delegation of amateurs who give

approval to Communist election victory

- Bush greets Iliescu at the UN in New York
- Bush sends aid to the Communist Government of Romania and prepares to grant MFN

After George Bush became President in January 1989, he continued the policy of supporting Ceausescu even though it was clear that Ceausescu was hated by virtually all Romanians. Demonstrations against the Ceausescu regime began in Timisoara in mid December 1989. Nicolae Ceausescu was removed from power on December 22, 1989, and he and his wife, Elena, were executed on December 25, 1989.

Subsequently much evidence makes it probable that a real revolution did not take place, but rather a coup d'etat led by Romanian Communists under the direction of (or at least in alliance with) the Soviet KGB and GRU (military intelligence). This is not to say, however, that thousands of courageous individuals were not taking part in demonstrations to help bring down the Communist government.

Ceausescu was apparently overthrown in a military-intelligence coup for which the Soviet KGB and GRU had planned many months if not years previously. The Soviets "conspired with a pro-Soviet clique in Bucharest to remove Ceausescu, using a 'popular' uprising as a screen, thereby creating the propaganda myth of Pravda . . . and The New York Times." [16] The ouster of Ceausescu was carried out to preserve Communist control in Romania. Any spontaneity of the "revolution" is refuted by several developments.

According to two former top officials of the National Salvation Front, Silviu Brucan and Nicolae Militaru, longtime conspirators had already gained the support of the army and most of the secret police before the demonstrations in Timisoara. Brucan and Militaru maintain that the plot to get rid of Ceausescu went back some 15 years, and that the "idea that [the army's] 180-degree change [in disobeying orders and siding with the demonstrators] was spontaneous is completely false." [17] But most astute observers agree that the Romanian Communist conspirators had prepared for the coup at least six months before Timisoara. General Militaru himself said on tape that the National Salvation Front Council had been functioning for six months. [18]

The main independent newspaper Romania Libera maintains that the NSF's detailed proclamation was too sophisticated to have been produced instantly; that the NSF stayed in close touch with the Soviet Embassy throughout the crisis; and that the key players in the instant front appeared immediately after the departure of the Ceausescus (as if on cue): Petre Roman, currently Prime Minister; Ion Iliescu, President; Nicolae Militaru, the first NSF Defense Minister; Victor Stanculescu, currently Defense Minister, and at least five others. [19]

Also when Ceausescu was captured, Iliescu was the first to announce the news from the balcony of the Central Committee building, where he remained in one place for the next two hours addressing the crowd under spotlights. No one fired at him, not even the Securitate which was supposedly loyal to Ceausescu. [20]

The coup was masterfully staged and televised to the world. The NSF "junta used the [Timisoara] incident (possibly exacerbating it deliberately, by provocation), skilfully distorted the reality and, by activating a contingency plan, engineered the coup of 22nd December." [21]

One of the most blatant cases of disinformation was the televised massacre of demonstrators in Timisoara, initially reported as numbering in the thousands. As the French writer Nicolas Peucelle put it: big brother understood "that to persuade the West, there must be televised pictures, all the more effective if televised live." [22] It was later reported by the Coroner of Timis County (Timisoara) Dr. Milan Dressler that the mass grave shown around the world with dozens of bodies supposedly gunned down by Ceausescu forces, actually was a pauper's grave with bodies in advanced stages of decomposition.

And the worldwide reports (wire reports, The Wall Street Journal, The New York Times, The Washington Times, etc.) of up to 12,000 killed in Timisoara and up to 70,000 nationwide were later revised downward to perhaps as many as 1,000 overall. [23]

The coup was superb, as Peucelle put it: *"masterfully planned and executed, and as usual the West understood nothing of the manipulation that concealed it."* (italics mine) [24]

It was not long before many Romanians and much of the world recognized Ion Iliescu and Petre Roman and their National Salvation Front for what it was and is: a continuation of most of the Ceausescu Government with different names and faces for the maintenance of the Communist system.

The NSF President, Ion Iliescu, was a life-long Communist and past Central Committee member. Iliescu started out as a Ceausescu loyalist and remained a privileged member of the Communist nomenklatura. Iliescu studied in Moscow for several years as a friend of Gorbachev. Iliescu was the head of foreign students at the University of Moscow where Gorbachev served as the president of Russian students.[25]

NSF Prime Minister, Petre Roman, was born into one of the oldest Communist families in Romania. His Jewish father who was originally named Ernst Neulander took the name Valter Roman. Petre Roman followed his father's footsteps into the Communist Party where he became very close to Zoia Ceausescu (the daughter of Nicolae and Elena). He has always been part of the nomenklatura or Communist Party establishment in Romania. [26] Almost all of the other principal members of the NSF executive are Communists who worked for Ceausescu in the past.

The NSF Communists moved quickly to assert their control over the traditional Communist levers of power: the military, secret police and Communist Party apparatus itself right down to the local level. "Many local and county-level Communist officials . . . simply changed hats. Now instead of sending reports to the party headquarters in Bucharest, they send them to the front," said the editor of the independent newspaper Romania Libera. [27] They made some "reforms" along the lines of Gorbachev's actions in the USSR: greater freedom of travel and emigration, increased contacts with the West, the beginning steps toward small scale private enterprise, and the "appearance" of political participation for non-communists.

Most freedoms were severely curtailed and restricted, and the new regime used the secret police to enforce its will and intimidate opponents. "Miners" (many of whom had been secret police agents planted in the Jiu Valley mines by Ceausescu) and other thugs were utilized by the NSF to frighten opposition to the Front. In February 1990 "truckloads and trainloads of aggressive factory workers and former Communist Party thugs" were brought in by Iliescu to intimidate anti-Communist demonstrators. [28]

Some of the best evidence of the Front's true colors came with the May 20, 1990, elections. Throughout the electoral campaign, the NSF controlled jobs, information, salaries, secret police operations and most aspects of life in the country. The major opposition could not get on television during most of the campaign because of NSF media dominance. The leading opposition newspaper (Romania Libera) had its copies destroyed on a regular basis by Iliescu's thugs.

Ion Ratiu and Radu Campeanu, the two leading opposition candidates were physically beaten up during the campaign; and two workers for the National Peasant Party were beaten to death. Leading opposition activists had their telephones tapped, received threatening telephone calls, and suffered harassment during the campaign. [29]

A Resolution on Romania proposed by the Senate Foreign Relations Committee Minority summed it up: "the NSF participated in the elections as a party and has used its dominant position to gain unfair advantage by using its control of communications, transportation, and access to media," while also carrying out "widespread intimidation and violence in the election campaign, including pro-Front mob attacks on opposition candidates and rallies . . . " [30]

Opposition electoral campaigning was systematically obstructed by the NSF which used television, radio and newspapers for its purposes. Campaign meetings were often broken up by force, and posters and campaign material destroyed. [31]

While the election was effectively stolen long before the actual balloting took place, election day violations and fraud were widespread. On election day, ballot boxes were stuffed, ballots were pre-stamped for the Front, secret police agents working for the Front monitored the polls and placed the ballots in the boxes, and secret ballot voting was usually not possible. [32] Howard Phillips, who observed the election at the invitation of the main opposition parties, reported that he himself witnessed widespread fraud at numerous polling places in and around Bucharest. Noting that NSF election monitors handled ballots, he observed that "in a country where going against the government can cost you your home, your job, your freedom, or even your life, it takes unusual courage for an impoverished peasant to risk voting against the NSF in such circumstances." [33]

Bush sent an election observer delegation headed by New Mexico Governor Garrey Carruthers, who was "not ready for prime time, as he declared to the world (contrary to extensive evidence adduced by a great many journalists and other observers) that the elections were free and fair." [34]

Ovidiu Opresco, American Romanian anti-Communist activist (who fled Ceausescu's Romania after suffering persecution and punishment for refusing to join the Communist Party) wrote in February 1991 that Bush's election delegation "gave a dishonest, white-wash report on the sham elections in Romania . . . which helps prove (along with sending an inept Ambassador who supports the Iliescu-Roman Communist regime and reports that the sham elections were fair) beyond any doubt that the intention of [the] Bush Administration is to help communists stay in power and not to encourage the restoration of democracy in Eastern Europe." [35]

The fraud was so bad and the Communist National Salvation Front stuffed so many ballots that more votes were cast than there were eligible voters. A free and fair election would hardly result in over 17 million votes cast when the electorate was only 16 million![36] Yet even when the evidence of Communist fraud was so obvious (you can't get more obvious than having 17 million votes cast by an electorate of only 16 million), Washington still "recognized" as fair the May 20, 1990, elections in Romania.

Bush's delegation called the election "free" and "enthusiastic" and State Department spokesman Richard Boucher said it was "an important beginning for Romania." [37]

When the White House and State Department lend U.S. credibility and support to such fraudulent elections held by the Communists, only one conclusion can be reached: they want the Communists in power!

The White House delegation and State Department statements which gave Washington's stamp of approval to the elections are all the more troubling when compared with other assessments. Lynn Boyer, who compiled the Report on the International Observer Delegation to the Romanian Elections, May 20, 1990, for the Senate Minority on the Foreign Relations Committee wrote that "my delegation was far more critical of the election process than the President's delegation. I would hardly call the process free and fair." [38]

Two European delegations said the balloting "had been compromised by voter coercion and intimidation in rural areas where 50% of the population resides." [39] One of them — a 25 observer team of West European conservative politicians — through their spokesman Andreas Khol said "there seems to have been a general pattern favoring the National Salvation Front, and intimidating people in the countryside to vote for the National Salvation Front."[40]

Howard Phillips with an independent American delegation said that "of course, the election was not free or fair." [41]

The National Peasant Party and the National Liberal Party (the two main opposition groups) strongly criticized the fraudulent nature of the election and issued lengthy reports detailing the stealing of the election by the NSF.

Not long after the sham elections which confirmed the NSF Communists in power, Iliescu ordered more government "vigilantes" into operation. On June 14th and 15th miners acting at the behest of the NSF brutally beat up political opponents peacefully demonstrating as well as innocent bystanders. Over 1,000 persons were arrested for simply exercising their fundamental right of free expression and association. Additionally the miners singled out as targets the offices of the opposition National Peasant Party and National Liberal Party. [42] (See PHOTO OF OFFICE)

A little more than a year after the fall of Ceausescu, the situation looks bleak for the cause of freedom and democratic government in Romania. The Communists are still in charge. The secret police is still operating much as before and the 1,000 or so secret police agents who were reportedly captured by the government have not been brought to trial. One knowledgeable and astute observer who lives in the western part of the country told me that many agents who previously operated in one city were simply transferred to another city where they are unfamiliar to the people. Telephones are still being tapped, and people are still being surveilled. Generally the revamped Securitate seems to be more subtle but nonetheless pervasive. [43]

Even the Intelligence chief Virgil Magureanu admitted that some 6,000 former Securitate officers had been hired by his new Intelligence service. [44] Emil Tatu, former President of the Romanian-American National Congress, summed it up in a letter of June 8, 1990, to President Bush (who cannot say he was not informed): "in Romania nothing is changed after the Revolution except the Despot. Everything else is the same; same terrorist gang composed of the old nomenclatura, communist-activists, securitate, militia, prosecutors, judges, chiefs of main news-media (radio, TV, newspapers) all of them headed by the new despot Iliescu, forming the communist monopoly of power, who, for 45 years, continue to maltreat the Romanian People." [45]

The political and economic situation has dramatically deteriorated for the people. Life has become more difficult for political opponents of the regime as well as for the remnants of the independent media. The opposition is so divided and weak that the new umbrella organization for much of the opposition (Civic Alliance) has expressed support for National Liberal Party leader Radu Campeanu's call for a coalition with the Communists. [46] Recently a prominent and well educated American of Romanian origin visited the country after a 23 year absence and described what he saw as "a trip to hell, beyond comprehension, with pervasive robbery and human degradation, and secret police control." [47]

In February 1991 World Press Review reported that "the National Salvation Front is treating opposition as traitors and using television as a propaganda tool. Once again, the press has been forbidden to speak the truth. Pro-government newspapers pour

BUSH ADMINISTRATION ENDORSES NEW COMMUNIST REGIME IN ROMANIA

"The National Salvation Front is the new legitimate government of Romania . . . founded on the democratic will of the people."

The White House, December 25,1989

COURTESY WORLD UNION OF FREE ROMANIANS

National Salvation Front "miners" vandalize the office of National Peasant Candidate Ion Ratiu. May, 1990

May 20,1990:

Bush Administration praises corrupt Romanian elections as "free."

venom against critics . . . Romania cannot boast a single genuinely independent newspaper or publisher, because all printing facilities are government controlled. Newspapers have become very cautious for fear of losing their right to publish at all." [48] Prices have increased more than two and one half times while wages have stayed the same. Food, especially meat, is scarce and expensive. [49]

One prominent Romanian told me in February 1991 that "Romanians are now free not to leave the country," explaining that before the NSF many could at least flee from the country as defectors or refugees, but that now other countries would not take them because of supposed freedom and non-persecution.

Despite the miserable situation in Romania and the continuing NSF control, the U.S. Government reaction has been supportive of the Communists.

The Bush-Baker policy has simply confirmed the response of Howard Phillips to Romania's honorable head of the National Peasant Party, Corneliu Coposu. When Coposu said that "for every day of the 17 and one half years he was in a Communist prison following World War II, he reflected on the Yalta betrayal of Romania by FDR and his adviser, Harry Hopkins," and now hoped that "George Bush and Baker would not repeat history by making another deal with the Communists — Gorbachev and Iliescu — at the expense of the Romanian people," Phillips advised him "not to count on the U.S. Government to stand with the people against the Communist Party of Romania." [50]

The Bush Administration immediately on December 23, 1989, announced recognition of and support for the NSF Communist Government. The U.S. was among the first countries to recognize the legimitacy of the post-Ceausescu government along with the Soviets whose spokesman proclaimed "full solidarity with the National Salvation Committee, the new supreme body of power in Romania, and with its platform." [51] For the Bush Administration, Marlin Fitzwater announced on December 25th: "The United States Government, with the full support of the American people, extends to the National Salvation Front congratulations on the re-establishment founded on the democratic will of the Romanian people." [52]

Other administration and State Department actions outraged freedom-seeking Romanians and boosted the Communists. Secretary Baker unbelievably announced that he would not mind if Soviet and Warsaw Pact troops went into Romania to assist the NSF presumably in defeating forces loyal to Ceausescu! [53] Pro-freedom and anti-Communist Romanians were appalled at the Baker invitation for Soviet troops.

From the Romanian perspective this encouraged Soviet intervention (without Romania's approval) in a country where the Soviets are resented as invaders and aggressors. In addition, there is the historical question of some 3 million Romanians living in the Soviet Moldavian province (where Romanians form a large majority) as a result of the Soviet annexation of Romanian Bessarabia (Moldavia) in 1940. The Soviets held on to the seized province after the end of World War II. In addition to the Soviets occupying a large chunk of Romanian territory, Romanians remember the Russians as the ones who forcibly imposed Communism on an unwilling people and country in the late 1940's. Thus for the Secretary of State or those advising him to be so ignorant of such an important nationalistic reality of Eastern Europe is shocking.

Equally appalling is the implication of inviting the unwelcome Soviet Communists into Romania when our policy should have been trying to get Soviet troops out of Eastern Europe. As John P. Roche put it: "To Russians, who have a historic fondness for spheres of influence, this sounded like a hunting license — a rerun of Khrushchev's reading of Dulles." [54] In other words when Khrushchev got the signal from John Foster Dulles that the U.S. was not interested in intervening in "internal" Soviet affairs,Soviet tanks rolled into Budapest, Hungary in 1956.

Just prior to the upheaval in Romania, Bush had appointed as U.S. Ambassador a major financial contributor and retired businessman from Portland, Oregon, Alan Green, Jr. In March of 1990 the Boston Globe reported that Green and his deputy, Larry C. Naper, almost alone in the embassy were supporting the Front as "a clear break from Ceausescu despotism." [55]

The naivete of Bush's Ambassador Green was made even more obvious during the May 1990 elections, when Green used every occasion to back the Front (even as it was stealing the elections). Howard Phillips who was in Bucharest at the time said that Green encouraged the Bush observer delegation head to "provide a clean bill of health for the continued incumbency of Romania's 'President' Ion Iliescu, Mikhail Gorbachev's comrade and protege, who heads the NSF, so that Occidental Petroleum can harvest Romania's crude oil, even as U.S. taxpayers (in the name of 'democracy') are forced to shovel in hundreds of millions of dollars to help entrench the post-Ceausescu Communist regime."[56]

The first anniversary of the fall of Ceausescu which should have been a time for celebration was instead a time of greater disillusionment. As a leading Romanian dissident put it a letter (of December 28, 1990) sent to me by courier, "the euphoria of December 1989 has given way to frustration and hopelessness." [57] He went on to say that "the May elections were rigged and the electoral campaign took place in profoundly undemocratic conditions. As usual, the western envoys turned a diplomatic blind eye to it. But the narrow-mindedness of the [opposition] political parties [is] lending an aura of democracy to an essentially undemocratic regime . . . However, nowhere in Europe except Albania is the old guard more deeply entrenched than in this country (Romania)." [58]

It was fitting that the same Bush who helped boost Ceausescu by visiting him in Bucharest also shook hands with Iliescu in New York on September 30, 1990 (not a formal meeting). Iliescu spent his days in New York at the UN and in wooing the U.S. Administration and corporate elite of the Establishment which has long done business with Communist controlled Romania. Iliescu met with Brent Scowcroft, Thomas R. Pickering (U.S. Ambassador to the UN), Henry Kissinger, Jewish leaders, and major businessmen.

It was also a sad spectacle to see some members of the Romanian ethnic community (many of these Securitate plants) including Graphic Artist Eugen Mihaescu, falling all over themselves to impress Iliescu (for business and /or other purposes). Other American Romanian church leaders had taken steps to work with Iliescu's Government by attending a Romanian Embassy function in Washington some months earlier. Apparently no lessons were learned from the overwhelming evidence of religious collaboration with Ceausescu's regime.

One tragic legacy of Communism in Romania (especially the Ceausescu years) is the willingness of so many individuals to sell their souls to the devil for money and personal advancement. Of course we have plenty of such individuals in America. The practice results more from a moral decline which has befallen Communist Romania and Capitalist America alike (if not to the same degree). As the current President of the Evangelical Alliance of Christians (Baptists, Brethren, Pentecostals, and Lord's Army of the Orthodox Church), Paul Negrut, put it while addressing 100,000 people in Oradea after the December 1989 upheaval "There is darkness and sorrow where there is no God." [59]

The Bush Administration has sent millions of dollars in "humanitarian" and medical aid to the Romanian Communist Government. [60] It is one thing to want to help those needy Romanians suffering, and it is another to send aid to the Communist Government to distribute such assistance. In fact, consistent reports have exposed the stealing by NSF supporters and secret police agents of medical and humanitarian aid sent to Romania. Christopher Walker reporting for The Times of London said that aid destined for the handicapped and others in need in Romania "has mostly been stolen by former communist party members" and it has been "happening all over Romania; it is going to the former party cadres, to the nomenklatura who share it out among themselves."[61]

Yet despite mistake after mistake, and sell out after sell out of the anti-communists in Romania, Washington has learned nothing. From every reliable source on Capitol Hill and among Romanians in the know, the Bush Administration is finalizing plans to grant the NSF Communist regime MFN and its attendant benefits. Bush, Baker, Green, and Carruthers have given aid and comfort to an enemy of freedom-seeking Romanians and an enemy of America. For this there is no excuse.

POLICY RECOMMENDATIONS INCLUDE:

- Withdraw recognition of the Communist NSF.
- Withhold Most-Favored-Nation treaty status from the Communist regime.
- Do not grant MFN, economic assistance, technology, or political support via high level visits to Romania until it elects a non-communist government in a free and democratic election; until it respects human rights; until it adopts a constitution and guarantees freedoms of speech, assembly, secret ballot voting, press (including the unhindered establishment of independent television, radio and newspaper-magazine operations), the freer practice of religion, free local and national elections, and other standard Western freedoms.
- Encourage Washington to express moral and political solidarity with the pro-freedom & pro-democratic, anti-communist groups in Romania who favor a free enterprise, non-socialistic economic system. Washington can use the instruments of Voice of America, Radio Free Europe, the United States Information Agency, and the Endowment for Democracy for such encouragement.
- George Bush should meet with the leading proponents of a Free and Non-Communist Romania rather than rely solely on Lawrence Eagleburger for advice on Romania. Some of these anti-Communists include: Father Calciu (in the U.S.), Corneliu Coposu, Doina Cornea, Ion Ratiu, Valentin Turcanu, and many student activists.
- Assist private groups and individuals in helping the beleagured anti-communists with publications, books, printing and copying tools, food and medicines, and above all spiritual guidance and comfort to those who are attempting recovery and restoration from a horrible nightmare of mental, physical and psychological destruction. Any such assistance should be routed through reliable individuals and groups totally separate from the current NSF Communist government.

New World Order: The End of American Sovereignty?

CHAPTER 6
BUSH'S NEW WORLD ORDER WITH THE SOVIETS IN THE UN

"with a new world order . . . struggling to be born . . . we are now in sight of a United Nations that performs as envisioned by its founders"

—George Bush to Congress, September 11, 1990

"I cannot see that any rational American . . . could conceivably try to fulfill the major national purposes of the United States through the United Nations. It would be comparable to the United States seeking to pass its legislation through the Supreme Soviet of the USSR"

—Charles Lichenstein, former Deputy Ambassador to the UN, writing in August 1986

Bush's New World Order has so quickly become an integral part of the major media lexicon in 1990 and 1991, that Bush's planners must have figured it could be safely projected to the general public. After all, six years of media preparation on Gorbachev's "pro-democratic" actions convinced most in the West that he had nothing in common with his Bolshevik predecessors. Similarly media saturation of the idea of Bush's genius in foreign policy convinced most that Bush had a legitimate, non-threatening (to America) grand design for world peace and world cooperation. The New World Order, then, is nothing more to most Americans than words for a Bush Doctrine in foreign policy. Most are not aware that the term "new world order" and plans for its implementation have been around for some time.

Because the New World Order has been presented to us as a desirable objective, few are aware of the harmful consequences. Thus all kinds of voices have been raised in support of it.

In conjunction with the American attack on Iraqi forces in January 1991, Bush emphasized the New World Order in a nationally television address and in his official letter to Congress in which he stated: "the administration made clear that there could be no reward for aggression lest we undermine prospects for an expanded constructive role for the UN Security Council and for a new, more peaceful world order."[1]

National Security Adviser Brent Scowcroft described the New World Order as a "defining moment in world history. The cold war is over. We have the prospect of incipient cooperation among the major powers who have an inordinate responsibility for both the rule of law and peace and security in the world. If we can establish in this case the role of the United Nations, the role of the Permanent Five, of the great powers, for the maintenance of an international order in the way that one should work to resolve disputes, then I think the next time it might be easier .... And the next time all it may take is a single UN resolution to solve the problem . . . "[2]

National columnists write interminably about Bush's New World Order as if it is the greatest thing we could do for mankind, and even the Reverend Billy Graham talked about it after staying with Bush at the White House during the early days of the Persian Gulf War. R. W. Apple Jr. of The New York Times describes the Bush foreign policy objective as aiming to "contain conflict that threatens its economic interests, rather than containing Communism, and toward a new multilateralism, based in considerable degree on the United Nations . . . [while] curiously dependent upon the old adversary, the Soviet Union."[3]

Even liberal writers have recognized — unlike Bush — that such a firm commitment to the New World Order with Gorbachev has led to looking the other way while Soviet troops attack the peoples of the Baltics. Robert C. Maynard in Oakland wrote that the Bush-Gorbachev New World Order may not in the future look so benign with muted criticism by Bush of Soviet military actions in

Vilnius to keep the questionable Soviet support in the Persian Gulf.[4] Joan Beck of the Chicago Tribune wrote that the New World Order seems on shaky grounds considering that "if the real issue is freedom, stability and peace in the post-Cold War world, why are we doing so little about the Baltic nations, which are struggling to break free from the Soviet Union after 50 years"? [5]

Billy Graham said in a sermon before the President on January 17, 1991: "perhaps, out of this war 'will come a new peace and, as has been stated by the president, a new world order.'" [6] Whatever Graham meant by promoting Bush's New World Order, it is no surprise to those who watched with sadness and bitterness as he played into the hands of virtually every major Communist leader (from Gorbachev to Deng Xiaoping to Ceausescu) in order to preach in Communist countries and play a role on the international stage.

Graham's visit to the harsh Communist world of Nicolae Ceausescu was effectively used by Ceausescu to enhance his international reputation and continue to get U.S. and Western assistance to carry out more terror and murders inside Romania. A samizdat open letter from a Romanian Baptist published in Religion in Communist Lands said that Graham's trip "had contributed towards the obtaining of 'most favoured nation' status" for Ceausescu's Romania, and that Graham had paid political homage to the Communist regime by prefacing his messages with political and social references which praised Ceausescu. [7]

Bush's New World Order is clearly the first major step on the road to one world government. As Bush himself has stated repeatedly in 1990 and 1991, he aims to "craft a new world order for the resolution of disputes." [8] It is the idea of collective security with the Soviets and Americans leading the way under UN auspices. This, despite the fact that the UN as a whole votes against U.S. interests 61% of the time.[9] The Soviets and Americans would cooperate to keep order and peace and to deter aggression. Bush said "I know the promise of a new world order if it is done right." [10] And that is why I am worried.

In addition to the Soviet co-partners with Bush in the New World Order of Persian Gulf activity, it seems that the Trilateral aspect of world domination has not been forgotten. The Director of the State Department's Center for the Study of Foreign Affairs forecast in a report released in December, 1990 that the next two decades would see global power dominated by the three triad blocs: the U.S., Japan and the European Community. [11]

Others have described the development of the New World Order as one of four or five great powers dominating world affairs via the instruments of organizations like the UN and global corporations. Bush's Deputy Secretary of State Lawrence Eagleburger put it this way: "the issue is whether three power centers — the United States, Japan and Western Europe — can manage this process of transition . . . . " [12] Others have hinted that the old ideas of sovereignty and nationality will be casualities of the New World Order, which will be dominated behind the scenes by the money managers: global corporations and financial power centers.[13]

It is important to note how identical Soviet views are to the Bush Administration's with regard to the New World Order.

Yevgeny Primakov, Member of the Presidential Council and Director of the Soviet Institute of World Economics and International Relations, explained the coordinated role of Bush and Gorbachev in the new game. Primakov said the development "of a new world order that, after the cold war, can insure stability, security, justice, and the creation of conditions for progress for all people" is the desired aim. [14] The degree of trust between the Soviets and Americans (especially Gorbachev and Bush at the Helsinki Summit) has been "unpredecented" in the bilateral relations, Primakov said. Echoing Bush's sentiments, Primakov said the Persian Gulf crisis "is a kind of laboratory, where our efforts to create a new world order after the cold war are being tested. These efforts must include the impossibility of imposing one's will on other countries and the right of any people to be free to choose its path of development and system of government. Unquestionably, the mechanisms of the UN should play a special and growing role in this process." [15]

Soviet Orwellian terminology has not changed one iota. And having propagandized the Western public to accept the idea of a reformed, civilized Soviet Union, apparently few were shocked by the hypocrisy of Primakov's declaration of the Soviets not imposing their will on others (free to choose their own governments) just as the Soviets were using troops in the Baltic republics, Moldavia, Armenia, and Georgia, to repress independence and self-determination.

The New World Order idea has been around for decades. Its grand design perhaps originated with the League of Nations and later gravitated to the United Nations. Its grand design was to create a "new global political and economic system to replace the existing one." [16] Today the UN with its most prominent promoters found in the Council on Foreign Relations is playing the key role in Bush's plans for the New World Order. [17] The problem with this was expressed by former Deputy Ambassador to the UN, Charles Lichenstein in a 1986 interview: "I cannot see that any rational American, and it doesn't really matter whether you are for or against President Reagan, could conceivably try to fulfill the major national purposes of the United States through the United Nations. It would be comparable to the United States seeking to pass its legislation through the Supreme Soviet of the USSR." [18]

George Bush in praising the United Nations — hotbed of KGB spies and Third World anti-American radicals — said "a hundred generations searched for an elusive path to peace," but now with a new world struggling to be born "we are now in sight of a United Nations that performs as envisioned by its founders." [19] The principal partner for the U.S. in the New World Order is the Communist Soviet Union. In addition to the Soviet-American "cooperation" in the Persian Gulf War against Iraq, the partnership was at work when the U.S. decided not to help the democratic Lithuanians seeking independence from Moscow, and when the U.S. deferred to Soviet interests in German reunification. When the Soviets decided to temporarily turn over part of East-Central Europe to the West-U.S. for their economic salvage job, the partnership was at work (of course Romania and Bulgaria were not part of the tactical retreat by the Soviets).

According to an official of the Council on Foreign Relations (CFR): "we have to stay at the table and get involved in a new game" even though the Cold War is over." [20] The new game is called The

New World Order, with the U.S. and the Soviet Union at the United Nations serving as brokers for the world's conflicts. Of course in such a new world order, a dominant influence would be wielded by the big banks, the major media elite, neo-communist academicians, and leaders of the Council on Foreign Relations and the Trilateral Commission.

Addressing Congress on September 11th following the Helsinki Summit with Gorbachev, Bush praised U.S. troops serving in the Persian Gulf and Saudi Arabia "in defense of principle and the dream of a new world order" (the Persian Gulf War presented "a rare opportunity to move toward . . . World Order"). [21] White House spokesman Marlin Fitzwater put it in these words: "What we're saying now. . . is that as this new world order is formed, as we see new cooperation between East and West, between the United States and Soviet Union in solving regional conflicts, that we believe we should be cooperating with the Soviet Union in the Middle East."[22]

If Bush's pronouncements regarding the New World Order do not make him a supporter of one world government, what would?

And Bush appointments to top posts in the foreign policy making departments of the U.S. Government have only confirmed this. One could hardly find greater advocates of globalism and one-worldism than Henry Kissinger's top proteges and former colleagues at Kissinger Associates, Lawrence Eagleburger and Brent Scowcroft. In fact Scowcroft said the Persian Gulf War should be used to "cement an unprecedented U.S.-Soviet relationship" with the United States and the Soviet Union working together.

Also Secretary of State Baker took the initiative to invite the Soviets to send military forces to the Gulf. [23] This was yet another indication of the total lack of concern for American security. We spend billions of dollars keeping our weapons and defense procurement secret. Then Baker invites the Soviets to have a first hand look at all our military technology! Unbelievable. Baker called for a "new regional security structure" in the Middle East, almost tantamount to a NATO-type alliance with Moscow as a partner. [24]

Some reports have suggested that a behind the scenes arrangement between Washington and Moscow included a deal for tacit Soviet support of the U.S. position in Saudi Arabia vis-a-vis Saddam Hussein in return for long range American development of Soviet oil and gas deposits and "guaranteed" energy supplies for the U.S. to reduce dependency on the Middle East supplies. In any event those benefitting the most from the arrangements were surely the David Rockefellers and other oil mogul friends of Bush who have long led the way in helping Soviet Communism survive.

Henry Kissinger of course works behind the scenes via his consulting firm and the Council on Foreign Relations. When I told The New York Times in January 1989 that Kissinger would "to a large degree be in charge of foreign affairs behind the scenes and this seems like a betrayal of the political revolution that put Reagan in office," Kissinger replied that he "found Funderburk's suggestion mildly amusing, but not true," as his "views on foreign policy are well known," and thus "I [Kissinger] don't need a conspiracy." [25]

And Kissinger's views are well represented and reflected through his longtime proteges and former aides, Eagleburger and Scowcroft.

But Kissinger also makes public pronouncements as often as he can on prime time television and in the major media to enhance his value to the establishment. In some of his articles and interviews his publicly expressed views regarding the New World Order can be discerned.

In an interview with Newsweek, Kissinger described a post-Persian Gulf War agenda. The biggest challenge, he said, will be to maintain the new balance of power of the New World Order. Such a New World Order would come from "a set of legal arrangements and be safeguarded by collective security, with peace maintained by global and regional balances of power." [26] Kissinger also mentioned the potential value of a UN role in peace conferences after such wars.

Dr. Henry Kissinger — described as one of the three most prominent writers for the Council on Foreign Relations and its Foreign Affairs journal (and the only American mentioned) — concluded in a report to the Trilateral Commission that "East-West relations have entered a new phase, and consequently we face a challenge that will shape the future of international relations for several decades." [27] The new phase is obviously the New World Order, a major step toward one world government. As Kissinger colleague (in the CFR) and Soviet-East European Affairs analyst Charles Gati put it in the same CFR Annual Report: "in Eastern Europe the interests of the two superpowers seem to be converging."[28]

Only to the Insiders could Soviet and American interests be considered similar. Only to the Insiders could the New World Order and one world government be considered our foreign policy goal.

Certainly a New World Order would not benefit the average patriotic, tax paying American like it would the powerful Insiders in the U.S. and the Communist bosses in Moscow. When Bush and Gorbachev talk about shared goals they are not talking about the preservation of the distinctive American way of life, which includes belief in God, the traditional family, individual worth and dignity, private property, and a representative constitutional republic. An atheistic, materialist, secularist Marxist-Leninist boss in Moscow and the American Insider leadership making decisions behind closed doors which affect the whole world in terms of diveying up resources and militarily policing areas of the world is scarcely the way to help preserve America's values and beliefs and principles.

In becoming part of the New World Order and gaining Western bailout support, the Soviets have turned to their tried and true methods of disinformation and deception. The West has long been a willing accomplice of Soviet Orwellian-speak. During the decades of what the Soviets described as communist democracy the West was content to accept Soviet propaganda. Now Soviet hardliners in Moscow can say without fear of detection by the naive West that they will be "resolutely supported by the leaders of world politics who no longer dread the USSR as a totalitarian superpower, but fear that fragments of the collapsing collossus could destablize the world order." [29] One astute analyst points out the "false semantic opposition created between the terrible state of 'chaos' and the wonderful state of 'order'" ("order" meaning repression in the Soviet lexicon). [30]

Unfortunately the State Department and the rest of the foreign policy establishment take Soviet words at face value and fall

AP/WIDE WORLD PHOTOS

Bush & Gorbachev at Malta: New World Order Collaboration.
December 3, 1989

for Soviet disinformation and deception. Referring to the need for "order and stability" in the Soviet Union, whatever the cost in individual liberties, a State Department analyst said "I get the impression that a lot of Soviets are saying, 'Let's get things calmed down.' And if it takes a little arbitrary justice to make life more stable, well, O.K." [31] So, a genius at Foggy Bottom feels the Soviets are justified in using military troops and secret police to beat heads on the streets of Soviet cities and in the Baltics. Unconscionable!

Analysts allied with the Insiders-CFR say that the "revolutions of 1989" in Eastern Europe destroyed the old political order that had existed since World War II. With the disappearance of the old order, a new security arrangement or a New World Order has been developed. What is now needed, they note, is to "understand the new arrangement, seek to shore it up against threats that could destabilize it, and set the groundwork for a long-term political order."[32]

The new system is to include Soviet-American cooperation, accelerated European Economic Community (EEC) integration, and United Nations leadership.

The long range goal of Communists has consistently been world government under Communist leadership. It is no mere coincidence that the Insiders centered in the CFR have also been advocates of world government. This means the end of American sovereignty.

United Nations treaties and conventions require the end of national independence. As Samuel Francis puts it: "UN treaties demand that the United States alter its laws to suit the demands of a foreign political body."[33] Brian Urquhart, former Under Secretary General for Special Political Affairs at the UN, writes that the UN should be granted expanded powers to "manage vast problems such as global warming, refugees, overpopulation, environmental damage and the eradication of hunger and disease," which would mean the end of separate nations governing their own citizens.[34] That is ultimately what the one-worlders have in mind for us, and why we must do all in our power to stop it.

THE SOVIET'S UNTRUSTWORTHINESS SINCE BUSH DECLARED THE N.W.O.

England's Economist magazine reported that in late February 1991 a senior White House official said "the days when Soviet foreign policy was ideologically driven are gone. That gives America opportunities to work with the Soviets that it did not have in the past."[35] Yet throughout the Persian Gulf War the Soviets made every effort to stake out their own pro-radical-Arab positions (of sympathy with Saddam Hussein's partners and allies) while overtly mouthing a solidarity with the U.S.-U.N. position. The Soviets constantly made statements to distance themselves from the U.S. by saying such things as Moscow does not support any effort to destroy Iraq, and Moscow is ready to mediate urgently needed peace talks. Of course, Moscow's last ditch efforts to end the war through their own negotiations and peace plan with Iraq helped expose their true colors.

Official Washington downplayed — if not covered up — the Dimitri Fulmanov episode. On January 4, 1991, the Soviet cargo ship Dimitri Fulmanov was seized on its way to a Jordanian port loaded with military weapons, explosives, and tank parts destined for Saddam Hussein in Iraq. Upon apprehending the ship, it became obvious that the tank parts on board the ship could only have been intended for the Iraqis because Jordan had no tanks of that kind.

The New York Times reported on December 17, 1990, that some 2,300 Soviet advisers continued to work in Iraq and that hundreds of Soviet specialists continued to work on military contracts to "maintain high-technology combat aircraft in the Iraqi Air Force and Air Defense network." [36] On February 13, 1991, Bill Gertz reported in The Washington Times that "more evidence surfaced yesterday indicating Soviet military advisers are assisting Saddam Hussein's forces in Iraq, although Soviet and US officials have denied it. Allied electronic eavesdroppers intercepted Russian voices communicating on Iraqi military radio channels over the past two days, the leftist French newspaper Liberation reported yesterday." [37] In addition, over $23.5 billion worth of military equipment was sold to Iraq by the Soviets between 1982 and 1989. Since Iraq was one of the biggest buyers of Soviet military hardware, the Soviets were anxious to preserve and protect their investment and supply.

Ted Koppel reported on ABC TV's Nightline on January 31, 1991, that a report maintained that the Soviets were supplying Iraq with satellite photographs of the Persian Gulf battlefield. Bill Gertz wrote in The Washington Times on February 4, 1991, that "Soviet advisers in Iraq provide Saddam Hussein's military with information about the times U.S. spy satellites pass overhead, U.S. intelligence sources said." [38] Another report indicated that the Soviet Ambassador in Iraq alerted Saddam Hussein hours before the American attack on Iraq (since Washington had unbelievably agreed to inform the Soviets beforehand of any such action).

Despite such reports, Bush refrained from criticizing Gorbachev or questioning Soviet motives. And Bush repeatedly thanked Gorbachev for his efforts to help end the war peacefully, despite all of the deceit from Bush's ally in the Gulf War and New World Order. However equally telling about Soviet trustworthiness as an ally in any New World Order, were Soviet military moves designed to help Saddam Hussein and to repress the Baltics while the U.S. was preoccupied. In addition to the use of military troops to kill Lithuanians and Latvians, Moscow "secretly" acted to continue assisting her longtime ally Iraq.

It should be added that while the Soviets were simultaneously crushing Latvia and Lithuania, Gorbachev was signing a new aid package for Fidel Castro, shutting down the small elements of an open press in the USSR, and solidifying the installation of KGB-hardliners in the government (i.e. the promotion of Boris Pugo the new Interior Minister to Colonel General as recognition of his success in a nationwide police crackdown). [39]

The Soviets have committed numerous violations of the INF treaty that we signed with Gorbachev and the Soviets. The Soviets have even violated the conventional forces agreement that the U.S. signed with Gorbachev.

And this man Gorbachev was the "trusted" new ally for policing the world and helping the U.S. via the UN ensure peace, freedom, and national self-determination for all peoples? It seems apparent that Bush's New World Order means that the application of a moral principle (opposing a dictator who commits aggression against a small neighbor) may only have the single application against Saddam Hussein. [40] Or perhaps there is another such isolated tyrant who puts New World Order interests of Bush, Gorbachev, and Deng Xiaoping in jeopardy.

But being in bed with Gorbachev and Deng Xiaoping has meant that Bush's New World Order will not apply any such moral principle when the tyrants and aggressors are Gorbachev and Deng themselves!

Recent developments in China, the Baltics, and the Persian Gulf, are reason enough to determine that the New World Order of Bush and Gorbachev under UN auspices goes contrary to the moral principles Americans have long held dear.

One of the major problems of any Insider-led "collective security" scheme is "that it glides over the question of who identifies the bullies — and who decides how to deal with them." [41] By giving a New World Order partner such as the Soviets equal say in identifying and dealing with "the bullies," Bush limits joint military actions to those against isolated tyrants like Saddam Hussein.

The Soviet Communists under Gorbachev are obviously a key element in Bush's plans. White House aides in mid March 1991 said they worry about the "chances that the Soviet Union's accelerating internal crackup could eventually outpace — and undermine — George Bush's bid to erect a new world order." [42]

The problem is that by joining with Communists, you have to split the differences between policies. But how can Americans back policies that are half-free and half-Communist?

By having Communist tyrants and other dictatorships (in the UN) as allies, Bush ensures that the unparalleled scourge of Communism will never be defeated, but rather assisted by America.

And such a New World Order alliance only guarantees that America's historic principles will be sold out.

CHAPTER 7

CONCLUSION: BUSH ADMINISTRATION APPEASEMENT PRECEDED THREE MASSACRES

BUSH ADMINISTRATION STATEMENTS:

Before the Tiananmen Square Massacre in Communist China:

"The [Communist] Government in trouble in China is a friendly government with which we have had good relations. We don't wish that government ill."

— State Department official, quoted in The New York Times, May 22, 1989

Before Iraq's massacre of Kuwait:

"We have no opinion on your border disputes with Kuwait"

— April Glaspie, President Bush's Ambassador to Iraq, to Iraqi Dictator Saddam Hussein, July 25, 1990

Before Mikhail Gorbachev's massacre of Lithuanians and Latvians:

"We're talking relatively small potatoes"

— White House official on the importance of the Baltics, late April 1990

On June 4, 1989, the Tiananmen Square Massacre took place in China. On August 2, 1990, the massacre and rape of Kuwait began. And on January 13 and 20, 1991, the massacres took place in Lithuania and Latvia, respectively.

A clear trend of appeasement by the Bush Administration is seen in the weeks and months preceding each massacre.

Before the massacres in China, Kuwait, and Lithuania-Latvia, the aggressors gave the Bush Administration plenty of advanced notice about their intentions.

This is a luxury not often found in foreign policy crises. Yet in all three cases, the Bush Administration failed to warn the aggressor that there would be serious consequences if force were used. Even worse, with a wink and a nod to dictators, the Bush Administration indicated through public statements that it would look the other way and carry on business as usual if force were used.

And in the cases of Lithuania-Latvia, and China, the Bush Administration did just that.

When Bush went to Beijing in February 1989 and failed to bring up the subject of human rights, he signaled the Communist Chinese dictatorship that human rights were not important enough to become a sticking point in U.S.-Chinese relations.

The Chinese students first seized Tiananmen Square on April 19, 1989 — six weeks before the infamous massacre on June 4, 1989.

The Bush Administration had six weeks to formulate a strategy: six weeks to let the Chinese dictators know that if they use force to crush the students, the U.S. Government will respond by taking concrete actions, including sanctions. Instead the Bush Administration did nothing; or worse, played into the hands of the Communist government.

The Bush Administration could have issued strong statements in support of the pro-democracy students to let the Communist Chinese Government know that there would be a strong U.S. reaction if violence were used to smash the students' aspirations.

In fact, members of Congress from Congressman Stephen Solarz (D-NY) on the left to Senator Gordon Humphrey (R-NH) on the right urged the President to express America's strong support of the students.

As columnist A. M. Rosenthal put it on May 19, 1989:

> "Sadly, President Bush so far has failed to put this country where it belongs — out front, as the great ally of the revolution flowing across China . . . Why the Administration's uneasy awkwardness, the quiet at the top? <u>It seems afraid of annoying the Chinese government</u>, an American pecularity not shared by the people in the Chinese streets."[1]

Mr. Rosenthal is exactly right. And the word for "seems afraid of annoying the Chinese Government" is **APPEASEMENT**.

The Bush Administration repeatedly expressed its sympathy for the Chinese Government in the weeks preceding the Tiananmen Square Massacre.

And the State Department put the administration on record in favor of keeping the Communist Chinese Dictatorship in power. "The government in trouble in China is a friendly government with which we have had good relations. We don't wish that government ill," said the State Department. [2]

That was a clear signal to the Chinese Government to do whatever they deemed necessary to stay in power.

And the Bush Administration backed up its words of appeasement with actions of appeasement.

Two weeks prior to the massacre in Tiananmen Square, the Chinese Government imposed martial law. But instead of punishing the Chinese Government for restricting freedom via martial law, the Bush Administration rewarded it.

Just eleven days after the Chinese Communist Government imposed martial law — in a clear signal that a violent military crackdown was coming — the Bush Administration granted China Most Favored Nation Trade Status.

The Bush Administration decision to grant MFN after the declaration of martial law made it clear to the Chinese that the American Government would continue business as usual regardless of what it did with the Chinese students.

So it killed them by the thousands on June 4, 1989.

As columnist A. M. Rosenthal wrote after the massacre:

> "All those mumbled arguments in Washington that strong American support for the students would annoy the Beijing regime and make it nasty — what mockery they are now."[3]

But the Bush Administration did not learn a thing from the failure of its appeasement of the Chinese Communist Dictators.

Just over a year later, in July 1990, the Bush Administration watched for two weeks as Iraqi Dictator Saddam Hussein amassed his forces along the border with Kuwait.

The Bush Administration sent its Ambassador to Iraq, April Glaspie, to meet with Saddam Hussein. But instead of warning Saddam about the consequences of invading Iraq, the administration tried to appease Saddam Hussein.

Ambassador Glaspie listened to Saddam's threats to invade Kuwait and then expressed sympathy for Saddam's position, saying:

> "I know you need funds. We understand that and our opinion is that you should have the opportunity to rebuild your country. But we have no opinion on the Arab-Arab conflicts such as your border disagreement with Kuwait." [4]

Glaspie could have told Saddam in no uncertain terms not to go into Kuwait or the U.S. would respond. But she didn't.

And as the world found out on August 2, 1990, Bush Administration appeasement had failed again.

Here's how Senator Alfonse D'Amato (R-NY) described the State Department's role in the weeks and months leading up to the Iraqi invasion of Kuwait:

> "We had a State Department that was a mealy mouthed group. Incredible. Do not think they do not share the blame. Right up until the final days. Oh. We see him [Saddam] moderating. I said 'Why?' Well, he's sending someone to the international convention on chemical weapons. I asked the question, was that to find out how he could use them better, more effectively." [5]

So the Bush Administration's appeasement policies had failed twice — once in China and once in Iraq.

Did the Bush Administration learn from the failure of its appeasement of Deng Xiaoping and Saddam Hussein? NO.

It committed the same grievous errors in the months leading up to Mikhail Gorbachev's massacre in the Baltics.

The Bush Administration made it clear to Gorbachev that keeping Gorbachev in power in the Soviet Union was much more important than the freedom of the peoples of the Baltics.

When the White House aide publicly said of the Baltics: "we're talking relatively small potatoes;" it was a clear signal to Gorbachev that he could do what he wanted in the Baltics and the Bush Administration would not respond.

So Gorbachev sent the tanks into Lithuania and slaughtered unarmed civilians.

There is one final parallel between the massacres in the Soviet Union and Red China that cannot be overlooked. Because it says a lot about George Bush's naivete in dealing with Communist dictators.

In the aftermath of both the Tiananmen Square Massacre and the Lithuania-Latvian Massacres, Bush actually believed that it was possible that Deng Xiaoping and Mikhail Gorbachev were not responsible.

Bush preferred to believe that his two favorite Communist dictators would not commit these atrocities.

Unfortunately none of the things Bush was praised for doing in the Persian Gulf War have been done in his dealings with Communist Dictators: no compromise with evil, the need to resist aggression, keeping America's word, and standing by those with a just cause. Instead, Bush has compromised with the evil Communist Dictators; he has not resisted Communist aggression or repression; he has not kept his word (e.g. to back Baltic independence); and he has not stood with those in the moral right like the Chinese students or unarmed civilians in the Baltics.

Bush's trust of Communist dictators like Deng Xiaoping and Mikhail Gorbachev has produced U.S. policies that have preserved Communist regimes at all costs and betrayed American principles of freedom, individual worth and dignity, and human rights, in the process.

By supporting Communist Dictators Mikhail Gorbachev, Deng Xiaoping, and Nicolae Ceausescu (and now his successor Ion Iliescu), rather than the people fighting for freedom in the USSR, China, and Romania, Bush has joined the very forces which are trying to take away our freedom.

Rewarding Communist dictators helps keep Communism alive.

And appeasing Communist dictators betrays America's principles.

There is a worldwide battle going on between freedom and slavery. And our leaders have opted to join forces with the enemies of freedom and with the enemies of America's republic.

It is thus our duty to oppose them with all of the resources at our disposal.

Because we consider the preservation of our faith, families, freedom and country to be our moral duty.

As Thomas Jefferson put it:

> "The time to guard against . . . tyranny is before they shall have gotten hold of us."

FOOTNOTES

CHAPTER 1: **BUSH'S FOREIGN POLICY TEAM**

1. "Mr. Consensus," Time, August 21, 1989, p. 22.
2. "A New Breeze is Blowing," Time, January 30, 1989, p. 18.
3. Roy Livesey, Understanding the New Age: World Government and World Religion (Chichester, England: New Wine Press, 1989), p. 187.
4. George F. Will, "Bush's Elitism Erases GOP's Appeal to Blue-Collar Democrats," The Washington Post in The Charlotte Observer, October 14, 1990, p.3c.
5. Time, January 7, 1991, pp. 29-30.
6. Ibid.
7. George Bush, Looking Forward: An Autobiography of George Bush (New York: Bantam Books, 1988), pp. 79, 79n.
8. Council on Foreign Relations Annual Report 1989, New York: July 1, 1988-June 30, 1989, pp. 105-106.
9. Ibid., pp. 178-199.
10. George Szamuely, "Lenin's Businessmen," National Review, January 28, 1991, p. 51.
11. Ibid.
12. "The Soviet Union Mourns Hammer," Reuters Report, December 11, 1990.
13. "Armand Hammer, R.I.P." Editorial, The Arizona Republic, December 13, 1990, p. A18.
14. Ronald Brownstein and Nina Easton, Reagan's Ruling Class: Portraits of the President's Top 100 Officials (Washington: Presidential Accountability Group, 1982), pp. 649-650.
15. Ibid., p. 647.
16. Jim Anderson, "The President's Man," Foreign Service Journal, December 1989, p. 32.
17. Martin Schram, "Geopolitics 'R' Us," The Washingtonian, February 1989, p. 274.
18. Jeff Gerth, "Rightist Conservatives Keep Eye on Kissinger," The New York Times, January 24, 1989, p. 14; and Elaine Sciolino, "Eagleburger Won't Disclose Kissinger's Client List," The New York Times, November 12, 1989.
19. Ibid.
20. David B. Funderburk, Pinstripes and Reds: An American Ambassador Caught Between the State Department and the Romanian Communists, 1981-85 (Washington: Selous Foundation Press, 1987), p. 135.

21. Brownstein and Easton, p. 550.

22. Ibid., p. 552.

23. Anderson, p. 36.

24. Who's Who in America 1984-85 (Chicago: Marquis Who's Who, 1984, 43rd edition, Vol. 2).

25. Funderburk, pp. 182-83. Simons recently served as a CFR International Affairs Fellow.

26. Thomas W. Simons, Jr., The End of the Cold War? (New York: St. Martin's Press, 1990), pp. 33,37, 65.

27. Ibid., 67.

28. Ibid., p. 183

CHAPTER 2: **APPEASEMENT OF DENG XIAOPING — THE BUTCHER OF BEIJING:** BUSH SAYS "DENG IS ONE OF PRE-EMINENT STATESMEN OF OUR TIME"

1. Steven W. Mosher, China Misperceived: American Illusions and Chinese Reality (New York: A New Republic Book-Basic Books, 1990), pp. 139-41, 154, 188, 193.

2. Alexandr Solzhenitsyn, The Mortal Danger (New York: Harper & Row Publishers, 1980), pp. 1-2.

3."Kissinger vs. Nixon," Time, December 25, 1989, p. 32. See also Dr. Jan S. Prybyla, "The Economic Consequences of Tiananmen Square," International Freedom Review, Volume 3, Number 1, Fall 1989, pp. 27-41.

4. Anthony Kubek, Modernizing China: A Comparative Analysis of the Two Chinas (Taipei: Caves Books, Ltd., 1987), pp. 13-15.

5. Ibid.

6. "Chinese Stole U.S. Secrets to Build Bomb," Knight-Ridder News Service in The News and Observer, November 22, 1990, p. 17A.

7. Where Do We Go From Here: A Blueprint for U.S. Aid to Emerging Democracies (Washington: International Freedom Foundation, 1990), p. 54.

8. R. W. Apple, Jr., The New York Times, February 27, 1989, p. 1A.

9. Ibid.

10. Ibid., p. A8.

11. "Beijing Stops Key Dissident From Meeting With Bush," The New York Times, February 27, 1989, p. A8.

12. Pei Minxin, "As Mr. Bush Partied in Beijing," The New York Times, February 28, 1989, p. I-23.

13. "More Exports to Red China," The New American, April 10, 1989, p.20.

14. The New York Times, May 21, 1989, p. A19.

15. Robert Pear, "The Utmost Caution," The New York Times, May 22, 1989.

16. The New York Times, May 14, 1989, p. A10.

17. Robert Pear, The New York Times, p. A21.

18. Howard G. Chua-Eoan, "The Wrath of Deng," Time, June 19, 1989, p.20.

19. The New York Times, June 20, 1989, p. A14.

20. White House Statement, June 20, 1989.

21. William Safire, "More Lying in State," The New York Times, December 25, 1989, p. 31.

22. Li Lu, Op-Ed, The New York Times, December 24, 1989, p. E11.

23. Ibid.

24. See Politics in America 1984 (Washington: Congressional Quarterly, 1983).

25. George J. Church, "Bush the Riverboat Gambler," Time, December 25, 1989, pp. 32-33.

26. Newsweek, December 11, 1989, p. 98.

27. Ibid.

28. Ibid.

29. "Tiananmen Square," The Washington Post National Weekly Edition, February 11-17, 1991, p. 29.

30. Church, p. 32.

31. "Appeasing Chinese Reds," The New American, January 1, 1991, p.8.

32. Mosher, p. 212.

33. "An Old China Hand Plays the China Card," U.S. News & World Report, December 25, 1989/January 1, 1990, p. 8.

34. Ibid.

35. "Tiananmen Anniversary," The New American, July 2, 1990, p. 17.

36. Church, p. 33.

37. Mary McGrory, "The Fog of Morality," The Washington Post, February 10, 1991, C1, C3.

38. Ibid.

39. James McGregor, "Two Dissidents, Adept at Raising Money, Get Longest Terms Yet in Beijing Trials," The Wall Street Journal, February 13, 1991, p. A9.

40. "A Tale of Two Tiananmens," The Economist, February 16, 1991, p.31.

41. Ibid.

42. "Protesters 'Cowards', Says Envoy to China," The News and Observer, December 3, 1990, p. 3A.

43. Richard L. Walker, The Human Cost of Communism In China: Senate Judiciary Committee Study (Washington: ACU Education & Research Institute, 1977).

44. "Deng's Real Deeds," The New American, January 15, 1991, p. 28.

45. Albert Jolis, "Bush and Gorbachev: The Flawed Partnership," Democracy Bulletin, Vol. 2, No. 4, Winter 1990-91, p. 2.

CHAPTER 3: **THE REAL GORBACHEV:** "I AM A CONVINCED COMMUNIST"

1. Patrick Buchanan, "Christmas is Merry for Bolsheviks," Dunn, N.C. Daily Record, December 28, 1990, p. 4; See also Anatoliy Golitsyn, New Lies For Old (New York: Dodd, Mead and Company, 1984), pp. 327-354.

2. Howard Phillips Issues & Strategy Bulletin #351 Special Edition, September 17, 1990, pp. 2-3.

3. "Food Aid for the Soviets" (Editorial), The Washington Post, November 18, 1990.

4. "The Myth of Gorbachev," Freedom At Issue, July-August 1990. See also the Intelligence Digest (London), Summer 1990.

5. Ibid.

6. "In the Words of Gary Kasparov," Democracy Bulletin, Vol. 2, No. 3, Fall 1990, p. 7.

7. Vladimir Bukovsky, "Gorbachev — An Assessment Update," Democracy Bulletin, Vol. 2, No. 4, Winter 1990/91, pp. 6-7.

8. The New York Times, October 16, 1990, p. A19.

9. Mikhail Gorbachev, Perestroika, quoted in Foundations of Liberty, Vol.2, Number 2, 1990, p. 110.

10. Canadian Digest, Vol. 2, No. 2, 1990, p. 1.

11. Sol Sanders, Living Off the West: Gorbachev's Secret Agenda and Why It will Fail (Lanham, Maryland: Madison Books, 1990), p. 191.

12. Ibid., p. 205.

13. Ibid., p. 207.

14. Foundations of Liberty, p. 92.

15. Ibid.

16. Mikhail Gorbachev, Perestroika (London: William Collins & Co., 1987), pp. 23,53. See also Canadian Digest, Vol. 1, No. 5, 1990, p. 3; and Dimitri Simes, "Gorbachev Plays Typical Leninist Game," Los Angeles Times, November 1987.

17. Lenin Letter to Politburo, March 19, 1922, cited in various publications including Christian Missions to the Communist World.

18. Canadian Digest, Vol. 2, No. 2, 1990, p. 2.

19. "Washington Whispers: Good Friends, Bad Timing," US News & World Report, December 10, 1990, p. 24.

20. Howard Phillips Issues & Strategy Bulletin #351 Special Edition, September 17, 1990, pp. 2-3.

21. Paul Bedard, "Bush Defends Power Grab By Gorbachev As Necessary," The Washington Times, December 28, 1990.

22. Warren Strobel and Martin Sieff, "U.S. Ready to Rush Aid to Reeling Soviets," The Washington Times, November 16, 1990.

23. Howard Phillips Issues & Strategy Bulletin #356, December 24, 1990.

24. Ibid.

25. "Washington Whispers: Glasnost Gets the Story," US News & World Report, January 14, 1991, p. 19.

26. Ibid.

27. Moscow Television Service in Russian, December 23, 1989, as reported by F.B.I.S. Sov. 1989-247, p. 81.

28. Marlin Maddoux, The Selling of Gorbachev (Dallas: International Christian Media, 1988), p. 21.

29. Golitsyn, New Lies for Old, pp. 327-339.

30. Edward Jay Epstein, Deception: The Invisible War Between the KGB and the CIA (New York: Simon and Schuster, 1989,), pp. 235, 272-79.

31. John Lenczowski, "A Dash of Skepticism Wouldn't Hurt," The Los Angeles Times, January 11, 1990.

32. Ibid. Also see John Rees, "How Moscow Tries to Manipulate Our National Elections, " Conservative Digest, March 1988, pp. 95-102.

33. Robert M. Gates, "A CIA Briefing on the USSR," Conservative Digest, December 1988, pp. 90-94.

34. Alan Stang, "Party Hack Under Her Silk Babushka," Conservative Digest, March 1988, pp. 61-63.

35. Ann Reilly Dowd, "What's Next for Bush," Fortune, March 25, 1991, p.40.

CHAPTER 4: **APPEASEMENT OF GORBACHEV IN THE BALTICS:** LITHUANIA'S PRESIDENT COMPARES BUSH'S POLICY TO "MUNICH"

1. "Lithuania: Past, Present, Uncertain Future," The Mindszenty Report, June 1990, Vol. 32, No. 6., pp. 1-2.

2. James J. Drummey, "The Captive Nations," The New American, July 14, 1986, p. 5.

3. Wilhelm Kahle, "Baltic Protestantism," Religion in Communist Lands, Vol.7, No. 4, Winter 1979, p. 223; Marite Sapiets, "Rebirth and Renewal in the Latvian Lutheran Church," Religion in Communist Lands, Vol. 16, No. 3, Autumn 1988, p.243.

4. Marite Sapiets, "Lithuanian Catholics Appeal to the Kremlin," Religion in Communist Lands, Vol. 12, No. 2, Summer 1984, p. 203.

5. "US Policy: The Baltic Republics," G.I.S.T., Bureau of Public Affairs, Department of State, August 1984.

6. Ibid.

7. "Gorbachev vs. the Baltics," The New American, June 18, 1990, p. 11.

8. "Lithuania: Past, Present, Uncertain Future," The Mindszenty Report, June 1990, Vol. 32, No. 6.

9. Richard Pipes, "The Soviet Union Adrift," Foreign Affairs, Vol. 70, No.1, 1990-91, p. 75.

10. "The Bush White House Fiddles While Gorbachev's Kremlin Fumes," U.S. News & World Report, April 2, 1990, p. 30.

11. "Has Bush Made the Right Choices?," Newsweek, April 23, 1990, p.32.

12. Ibid.

13. Albert Jolis, "Munich - Yalta -Vilnius," Democracy Bulletin, Vol. 2, No. 2, Summer 1990, pp. 1, 11.

14. Ibid.

15. George F. Will, "Bush: Read My Polls: If Lithuania's Liberty Is Sold to 'Save' Gorbachev, What Is Not For Sale?," Newsweek, May 7, 1990, p. 76.

16. Ibid.

17. Ibid. See also, "The Rising Heat of Lithuania, the Lingering Cool of Washington," US News and World Report, April 30, 1990, p. 32.

18. "Has Bush Made the Right Choices?"

19. "We Too Want To Be Free," The New American, July 31, 1989, pp. 18-19. Viktor Nakas of the Lithuanian Information Center in the U.S. clearly stated the end result of Bush's hands off policy: "The president is doing exactly what the Soviets want him to do. Essentially by doing nothing Tuesday, he is telling Gorbachev he has a free hand in Lithuania" ("Hands-off Policy Will Make Things Worse," USA Today, April 25, 1990, p. 11A).

20. "Lithuania: Past, Present, Uncertain Future."

21. "The Bush White House Fiddles While Gorbachev's Kremlin Fumes," p. 30.

22. Will, p. 76.

23. "How Gorby Took the Money — Before Bashing the Baltics," Business Week, February 4, 1991, p. 66.

24. "Investors Are Shaken — But Nobody's Packing," Business Week, January 28, 1991, p. 43.

25. "Soviets Set Curfew in Lithuania," The News and Observer, January 14, 1991, p. 5A.

26. "'The Tanks Hesitated, Then Lurched Forward . . .,'" Business Week, January 28, 1991, p. 44.

27. Bill Keller, The New York Times News Service in The News and Observer, January 13, 1991, p. 3A.

28. Christopher Connell, "Bush Condemns Soviet Use of Force," The News and Observer, January 14, 1991, p. 5A.

29. Bryan Brumley, "Colonel's Stands Reflect Contradictions," The News and Observer, February 4, 1991, p. 2A.

30. Don Oberdorfer, "Bush Remains Cautious on Baltic Events," The Washington Post, January 12, 1991; See also "Bloodshed in Lithuania," Newsweek, January 21, 1991, p. 41.

31. Albert Jolis, "Bush and Gorbachev: The Flawed Partnership," Democracy Bulletin, Vol. 2, No. 4, Winter 1990/91, pp. 1-2.

32. "President Bush's Statements on Massacre in Lithuania," Reuters, White House, January 13, 1991.

33. "Back to Iron Fists and Brazen Lies," Business Week, January 28, 1991, p. 41.

34. Rowland Evans and Robert Novak, "Bush's Blind Eye and the Baltics," The Washington Post, January 28, 1991, p. A11.

35. Oberdorfer, "Bush Remains Cautious on Baltic Events."

36. Tunne Kelam and Mari-Ann Rikken, "Selling Out the Baltics," The New York Times, January 8, 1991.

37. David S. Broder, "Timidity On the Baltics," The Washington Post, January 27, 1991, p. C7.

38. Douglas Stanglin, "Reaping the Whirlwind," US News and World Report, January 28, 1991, p. 54.

39. The Statement of Dainis Ivans, Vice President of the Supreme Council of the Republic of Latvia, Washington, January 22, 1991.

40. Ibid.

41. Senator Robert Dole on CNN's Larry King Live, February 26, 1991.

42. Congressional Record, U.S. Senate, January 4, 1991.

43. Congresswoman Patricia Schroeder, "We Must Work as Hard as We Can Toward Peace," The Congressional Record — House of Representatives, January 14, 1991, H 490.

44. Mark Louis Croatti Letter to the Editor, US News and World Report, February 4, 1991.

45. "Czechs Plan to Establish Lithuanian Ties," Los Angeles Times in The News and Observer, February 16, 1991, p. 12A.

46. John Budris Letter "Iceland Puts the West to Shame on Baltics," The New York Times, February 4, 1991.

47. Ibid.

48. Jeri Laber, "The Baltic Revolt," The New York Review of Books, Vol. 38, No. 6, March 28, 1991, p. 60.

49. Ibid., p. 62.

50. M. Stanton Evans, "What About Soviet Aggression in the Baltics?," Human Events, January 26, 1991.

CHAPTER 5: **APPEASEMENT OF NICOLAE CEAUSESCU IN ROMANIA:** BUSH VISITS CEAUSESCU AND SUPPORTS U.S. AID TO COMMUNISTS

1. See Dinu C. Giurescu, "Romania: The Protracted Struggle," Democracy Bulletin, Vol. 2, No. 4, Winter 1990-91, pp. 9-10. Examples of those killed include Roman Catholic priest Geza Palfi, Baptist pastor Sabin Teodosiu, and religious activists Traian Bogdan and Daniel Pausan (see Pinstripes and Reds, pp. 70-71).

2. Telephone Conversation with Father Calciu, February 18, 1991.

3. "To the U.S. With Love," US News & World Report, June 25, 1990, p.20.

4. Lumea Libera (New York), January 12, 1991, p. 1; and Newsweek,

5. Dinu C. Giurescu, The Razing of Romania's Past, International Preservation Report, New York: World Monuments Fund, 1989, pp. 47-50, 67-68.

6. See Kentucky State Senate Resolutions Boycotting Romanian Products, 1982, 1984.

7. Giurescu, The Razing of Romania's Past, p. 48.

8. Ion Mihai Pacepa, Red Horizons: Chronicles of A Communist Spy Chief (Washington: Regnery Gateway, 1987), p. 375.

9. Giurescu, "Romania: The Protracted Struggle," p. 9.

10. Nicholas Dima, Journey to Freedom (Washington: Selous Foundation Press, 1989), p. 343.

11. Pacepa, p. 375.

12. Giurescu, "Romania: The Protracted Struggle," p. 9. See also George Ross, Romania—Whither Now?, unpublished manuscript, July 1990, London.

13. Pinstripes & Reds, pp. 121-122.

14. Testimony of Governor Milton J. Shapp Before the Subcommittee on Trade Committee on Ways and Means, U.S. House of Representatives, June 12-13, 1982; See also Press Release from Milton J. Shapp, former Governor of Pennsylvania, July 9, 1982.

15. Nicholas Dima, pp. 344-345.

16. Lev Navrozov, "A Military Coup Backed by the KGB and GRU Ousted Ceausescu," New York City Tribune, January 10, 1990.

17. Marc Champion, "Romanian Revolution Depicted as Planned Coup, Not Uprising," The Washington Post, August 24, 1990, p. A19.

18. Navrozov.

19. Peter Keresztes, "Darker Forces Behind Romania's 'Front'," The Wall Street Journal, May 11, 1990.

20. Richard A. Tendler, "Soviets Ousted Ceausescu to Save Communist Party, West Watch, July-August 1990, p. 8.

21. George Ross, Romania-Whither Now?, unpublished manuscript, July 1990, London.

22. Nicolas Peucelle, "Romania's Puppet Revolution," Soldier of Fortune, July 1990, p. 51.

23. Joseph A. Reaves, "Coroner: Romanian Massacre Never Happened," Chicago Tribune, March 13, 1990, pp. 1, 6. See also "The Butcher of Timisoara," The Wall Street Journal, December 21, 1989; "Rampage in Romania," The New York Times, June 15, 1990, p. A14; Colin McIntyre, "Romania Massacre Toll Put at 2,000," The Washington Times, December 20, 1989, A1, A8; Dusan Stojanovic, "More Fighting After Army Claims Control-5,000 Reported Dead Since Friday," Associated Press Wire Report (New York), December 24, 1989; Radek Sikorski, "Christmas Day in Rumania, National Review, January 22, 1990, p. 24.

24. Peucelle, p. 55.

25. "A Man Who Could Become Rumania's Leader," The New York Times, December 12, 1989.

26. David Binder, "An Aristocrat Among the Revolutionaries," The New York Times, December 27, 1989.

27. Mary Battiata, "Anger at a Revolution Betrayed," The Washington Post, June 16, 1990.

28. Ibid.

29. David Funderburk, "Romanian Election Stolen," The New American, June 18, 1990, p. 16.

30. Resolution on Romania, U.S. Senate Committee on Foreign Relations Republican Staff, S. Con. Res. 131, June 22, 1990. See also Report on the International Observer Delegation to the Romanian Elections, May 20, 1990, prepared by Lynn Boyer.

31. Uniunea Mondiala A Romanilor Liberi (World Union of Free Romanians) Election Report, June 4, 1990, London.

32. Ibid.

33. Howard Phillips Issues and Strategy Bulletin # 336, June 4, 1990, Vienna, Virginia.

34. Ibid.

35. Letter to the author from Ovidiu Opresco, February 16, 1991, New York, NY.

36. "Romania's Urgent Need is Foreign Investment," The Free Romanian (London), November 1990, Vol. 6, No. 11.

37. Mary Battiata, "Validity of Romanian Election Disputed," The Washington Post, May 22, 1990, p. A17.

38. Lynn Boyer, "Report on the International Observer Delegation to the Romanian Elections, May 20, 1990," United States Senate, Committee on Foreign Relations (Minority), with attached letter, received by the author June 7, 1990.

39. Battiata, "Validity of Romanian Election Disputed, p. A17.

40. Ibid.

41. Howard Phillips Issues and Strategy Bulletin, June 4, 1990, p. 1.

42. "Question Mark Hangs Over West's Aid to Romania," The Free Romanian (London), July-August 1990, Vol. 6, No. 7-8.

43. Stephen Engelberg, "Uneasy Romanians Are Asking: Where Have All the Secret Agents Gone?," The New York Times, February 13, 1991, p. A4.

44. John Borrell, "If At First You Don't Succeed...," Time, January 7, 1991, p. 64.

45. Letter from Emil Tatu to President George Bush, June 8, 1990, Reseda, California.

46. Ibid.

47. A telephone conversation with a Romanian American friend in Washington, January 21, 1991.

48. "Romania," World Press Review, February 1990, p. 60.

49. See for example, Don Kyer, "The Romanian Revolution—A Year Later," Frontline Fellowship Newsletter, January 1991.

50. The Howard Phillips Issues and Strategy Bulletin, June 4, 1990, p. 2.

51. "Top Diplomats Support Rebellion in Bucharest," The Washington Post, December 24, 1989.

52. "New Romanian Government," The New American, January 29, 1990, p. 12.

53. "Ambassador Funderburk on Ceausescu Overthrow," Human Events, January 6, 1990, p. 3. See John P. Roche, "Lithuania: Death on the Installment Plan," National Review, April 30, 1990, pp. 32-33.

54. Roche, "Lithuania: Death on the Installment Plan," pp. 32-33.

55. "Crossed Signals," The Boston Globe, March 25, 1990.

56. The Howard Phillips Issues and Strategy Bulletin, June 4, 1990, p. 1.

57. Letter from leading Romanian dissident in Bucharest (dated December 28, 1990) sent to the author via courier.

58. Ibid.

59. "Working For Freedom," Frontier (Keston College, England), May-June 1990, pp.6-7.

60. See for example, "$500,000 in U.S. Aid Going to Romania," The Washington Times, December 27, 1989.

61. "Officials Steal Children's Aid," The Free Romanian (London), September 1990, Vol. 6, No. 9.

CHAPTER 6: **BUSH'S NEW WORLD ORDER WITH THE SOVIETS IN THE UN**

1. "Excerpts from Bush letter on the Gulf," The Washington Post, January 18, 1991, p. A19.

2. U.S. News & World Report, December 24, 1990, p. 27.

3. R. W. Apple Jr., "The New Order: Peace Isn't So Simple as the End of Cold War," The New York Times, November 25, 1990, p. 4A.

4. Robert C. Maynard, "Bush, Gorbachev Face a Long Morning After," Universal Press Syndicate in The News & Observer, January 18, 1991, p.13A.

5. Joan Beck, "A Ray of Hope for A New World Order," Chicago Tribune in The News & Observer, January 18, 1991, p. 13A.

6. Megan Rosenfeld, "Billy Graham, Hands On," The Washington Post, January 18, 1991, p. C-3.

7. "Reflections on Billy Graham's Trip to Romania, Religion in Communist Lands (Keston College, England), Summer 1986, Vol. 14, No. 2, pp. 224-226.

8. The Economist, January 5, 1991, p. 20.

9. See United Nations Voting Record, 1985 U.N. General Assembly Fortieth Session, (Washington: Selous Foundation, Vol. 1, 1987), pp. 1-4.

10. Time, January 7, 1991, pp. 20, 32-33.

11. "The New World Order-Scholar's Crystal Ball Provides Glimpse at Strange Alignment of World Power," The News and Observer, December 29, 1990, p. 11A.

12. "The New World Order-Arms Race Gives Way to Economics in Reshaping World," The News and Observer, December 1990, p. 10A.

13. Ibid.

14. Interview with Yevgeny Primakov "The Superpowers' New Rules," in World Press Review, December 1990, p. 14.

15. Ibid., p. 16.

16. Michael Collins Piper, "Who's Behind the 'New World Order'"?, The Spotlight Special Report in Boian News Service, New York, October-December 1990, B-3, B-4.

17. Ibid.

18. Charles Lichenstein, "United Nations", Common Sense, August, Vol.II, 1986.

19. "I Can Call Spirits From the Vasty Deep," The Economist, September 15, 1990, p. 29.

20. Patrick Buchanan, "It's Last Hurrah of the Globalists," The Daily Record, September 26, 1990, p. 4A.

21. James J. Drummey, "Bush's New World Order," The New American, October 8, 1990, p. 14.

22. Ibid.

23. Newsweek, September 17, 1990, pp. 25-26.

24. Ibid., p. 23.

25. Jeff Gerth, "Rightist Conservatives Keep Eye on Kissinger," The New York Times, January 24, 1989, p. 14.

26. Henry A. Kissinger, "A Postwar Agenda," Newsweek, January 28, 1991, pp. 44-46.

27. Council on Foreign Relations Annual Report, July 1, 1988-June 30, 1989, New York, 1989, p. 20.

28. Ibid.

29. Stephen Aubin, "What's Wrong With Chaos? And Who Says Soviet Order Will Be Better?," Defense Media Review (Boston University), December 1990, Vol. IV, No. 8, p. 3.

30. Ibid.

31. John Kohan, "New World Order? Or Law And Order?," Time, February 11, 1991, p. 58.

32. James A. Thomson, "European Security in the 1990's and the American Presence in Europe," United States-Soviet and East European Relations: Building a Congressional Cadre: The Aspen Institute: Queenstown, MD, 1990, pp.29-32.

33. Samuel Francis, "Son of New World Order," The Washington Times, October 24, 1990.

34. Ibid.

35. "New world order: What's new? Which world? Whose orders?," The Economist, February 23, 1991, p. 25.

36. The New York Times, December 17, 1990.

37. Julia Ackerman and Stephen Aubin, "Diplomacy Fails," Defense Media Review, February 28, 1991, Vol. 4, No. 10, p. 5.

38. Ibid.

39. "Gorbachev Promotes Hard-Line Police Chief," The New York Times News Service in The News and Observer, February 5, 1991, p. 6A.

40. George Will, "On A Clear Day, You Can See The New World Order," The News and Observer, February 4, 1991, p. 9A.

41. Mark Whitaker, "A Wrinkle in the New World Order," Newsweek, March 4, 1991, p. 51; and Carla Anne Robbins, "Is There A New World Order?," U.S. News and World Report, March 11, 1991, p. 50.

42. Paul Hofheinz, "On the Ropes?," Fortune, March 25, 1991, p. 64.

CHAPTER 7: **CONCLUSION:** BUSH ADMINISTRATION APPEASEMENT PRECEDED THREE MASSACRES

1. A. M. Rosenthal, "The Absent Americans," The New York Times, May 19, 1989, p. A35.

2. Robert Pear, "The Utmost Caution," The New YorkTimes, May 22, 1989.

3. A. M. Rosenthal, "Beijing and Moscow," The New York Times, June 6, 1989, p. A31.

4. "The Search for Scapegoats," Newsweek, October 1, 1990, pp. 24-25; Bruce W. Nelan, "Who Lost Kuwait?," Time, October 1, 1990, p. 54; and Face to Face with Connie Chung, CBS-TV, February 11, 1991.

5. Congressional Record, U.S. Senate, January11,1991, S233.

INDEX

ACKNOWLEDGEMENTS

The publication of this work was made possible in large measure by the early support and encouragement of Mr. Ben D. Robinson, Jr. through his Larry McDonald Foundation in St. Augustine, Florida.

If America is great because America is good it has certainly been blessed through the years to have patriotic individuals who put their country and its distinctive constitutional republic first. One such outstanding individual is Ben D. Robinson, Jr. His life has been devoted to educating America's youth about the dangers facing our republic, both foreign and domestic. He has placed patriotic books in high school and college libraries and granted scholarships to outstanding students who demonstrate a superior understanding of our cherished heritage. Mr. Robinson established Larry McDonald Scholarships for students who write winning essays based in large measure on W. Cleon Skousen's The Five Thousand Year Leap, and Catherine Bowen's Miracle of Philadelphia, and which are supportive of the traditional interpretation of the U.S. Constitution. Mr. Robinson named the scholarships and his foundation after Dr. Larry McDonald, the only U.S. Congressman to have served nine years and have a 100 per cent voting record for Constitutional government every year. Congressman Larry McDonald, America's leading anti-Communist, was killed when the Soviets ruthlessly shot down KAL 007 in the fall of 1983.

It has been a special honor and privilege for me to know Ben D. Robinson, Jr. during the past few years. He has been accurately described as a great patriot and great American by the late Congressman Larry McDonald and by former New Hampshire Governor Meldrim Thomson. Inasmuch as Communism is not dead, and our constitutional republic is still endangered by enemies in our very midst, I am especially grateful to Mr. Robinson for his efforts to save our great country.

David Tyson's assistance was indispensable in the writing and revisions of this book. His patience, hard work, and creative ideas, helped make my manuscript more understandable and more focused. For his interest and dedication to the worldwide struggle for freedom and conservative values in America, he is to be highly commended. I feel especially fortunate for his excellent help with this book. And I am indeed grateful for his long-standing friendship.

I am grateful for the indispensable help of my wife and partner, Betty. Without her help in so many ways, I would never have been able to complete this book. In addition to the research assistance and proof-reading she provided, she was as ever supportive and equally determined that this information be published for as many Americans as possible to see. Her support means more than I can say.

- -

BETRAYAL OF AMERICA

Bush's Appeasement of Communist Dictators
Betrays American Principles

by Former U.S. Ambassador to Romania
David B. Funderburk

1copy. . . . . $8.95 . . . . (+ $2 postage & handling)
50 copies. . . . . $300.00 . . . . . (+ $15 postage & handling)
100 copies. . . . . $500.00 . . . . . (+ $15 postage & handling)

I am enclosing a check or money order to:

BETRAYAL OF AMERICA
PO BOX 1124
DUNN, NC 28335

Name ______________________________

Address ______________________________

City ______________________________

State ______________ Zip ______________

BETRAYAL OF AMERICA

Bush's Appeasement of Communist Dictators Betrays American Principles

"An expert on the subject of no-win diplomacy who served during part of the Reagan administration as our Ambassador to Romania, tells about the betrayal of America. In his volume Ambassador Funderburk tells us that appeasement is leading America to an abattoir where liberty and freedom are slaughtered."

— **Meldrim Thomson, Jr.**
Former Governor of New Hampshire

"Ambassador David Funderburk is an American patriot of extraordinary courage, integrity, and discernment who represented the United States with great distinction as Ronald Reagan's Ambassador to Communist Romania . . . Instead of safeguarding U.S. national autonomy and defending the vital interests of our citizens, our government has rejected even a moral alliance with innocent people struggling for liberty in the Baltics, preferring instead to transfer our resources, our technology, and our moral capital to Marxist-Leninist despots in China, the USSR, and too many other places. Ambassador Funderburk provides an invaluable account which adds to his consistent far-sighted warnings regarding Communist deception and duplicity and the tragedy of our government's collaboration with the very forces which seek to deprive us of our freedom . . . It is a compelling account by one who has witnessed the betrayal of our nation by persons entrusted with its care."

— **Howard Phillips**
Chairman, The Conservative Caucus

"An outstanding book full of tangible evidence of the instrumentalities used by President Bush to promote the goals of a "New World Order."

— **Andrew J. Gatsis**
Brigadier General, U.S. Army (Ret.)

"Many others among us know the players and know the score, but Ambassador Funderburk is one of the few with the courage, integrity, and patriotism to tell it like it was, and is, and to tell us, straight from the shoulder, what we can and must do about it."

— **Tom Anderson**
Author & Former Presidential Candidate, American Party

BETRAYAL OF AMERICA

Bush's Appeasement of Communist Dictators Betrays American Principles

"An expert on the subject of no-win diplomacy who served during part of the Reagan administration as our Ambassador to Romania, tells about the betrayal of America. In his volume Ambassador Funderburk tells us that appeasement is leading America to an abattoir where liberty and freedom are slaughtered."

— **Meldrim Thomson, Jr.**
Former Governor of New Hampshire

"Ambassador David Funderburk is an American patriot of extraordinary courage, integrity, and discernment who represented the United States with great distinction as Ronald Reagan's Ambassador to Communist Romania . . . Instead of safeguarding U.S. national autonomy and defending the vital interests of our citizens, our government has rejected even a moral alliance with innocent people struggling for liberty in the Baltics, preferring instead to transfer our resources, our technology, and our moral capital to Marxist-Leninist despots in China, the USSR, and too many other places. Ambassador Funderburk provides an invaluable account which adds to his consistent far-sighted warnings regarding Communist deception and duplicity and the tragedy of our government's collaboration with the very forces which seek to deprive us of our freedom . . . It is a compelling account by one who has witnessed the betrayal of our nation by persons entrusted with its care."

— **Howard Phillips**
Chairman, The Conservative Caucus

"An outstanding book full of tangible evidence of the instrumentalities used by President Bush to promote the goals of a "New World Order."

— **Andrew J. Gatsis**
Brigadier General, U.S. Army (Ret.)

"Many others among us know the players and know the score, but Ambassador Funderburk is one of the few with the courage, integrity, and patriotism to tell it like it was, and is, and to tell us, straight from the shoulder, what we can and must do about it."

— **Tom Anderson**
Author & Former Presidential Candidate, American Party

BETRAYAL OF AMERICA

Bush's Appeasement of Communist Dictators
Betrays American Principles

by Former U.S. Ambassador to Romania
David B. Funderburk

1copy. . . . . $8.95 . . . . (+ $2 postage & handling)
50 copies. . . . . $300.00 . . . . . (+ $15 postage & handling)
100 copies. . . . . $500.00 . . . . . (+ $15 postage & handling)

I am enclosing a check or money order to:

BETRAYAL OF AMERICA
PO BOX 1124
DUNN, NC 28335

Name ____________________

Address ____________________

City ____________________

State ____________ Zip ____________

BETRAYAL OF AMERICA

Bush's Appeasement of Communist Dictators Betrays American Principles

"An expert on the subject of no-win diplomacy who served during part of the Reagan administration as our Ambassador to Romania, tells about the betrayal of America. In his volume Ambassador Funderburk tells us that appeasement is leading America to an abattoir where liberty and freedom are slaughtered."

— **Meldrim Thomson, Jr.**
Former Governor of New Hampshire

"Ambassador David Funderburk is an American patriot of extraordinary courage, integrity, and discernment who represented the United States with great distinction as Ronald Reagan's Ambassador to Communist Romania . . . Instead of safeguarding U.S. national autonomy and defending the vital interests of our citizens, our government has rejected even a moral alliance with innocent people struggling for liberty in the Baltics, preferring instead to transfer our resources, our technology, and our moral capital to Marxist-Leninist despots in China, the USSR, and too many other places. Ambassador Funderburk provides an invaluable account which adds to his consistent far-sighted warnings regarding Communist deception and duplicity and the tragedy of our government's collaboration with the very forces which seek to deprive us of our freedom . . . It is a compelling account by one who has witnessed the betrayal of our nation by persons entrusted with its care."

— **Howard Phillips**
Chairman, The Conservative Caucus

"An outstanding book full of tangible evidence of the instrumentalities used by President Bush to promote the goals of a "New World Order.""

— **Andrew J. Gatsis**
Brigadier General, U.S. Army (Ret.)

"Many others among us know the players and know the score, but Ambassador Funderburk is one of the few with the courage, integrity, and patriotism to tell it like it was, and is, and to tell us, straight from the shoulder, what we can and must do about it."

— **Tom Anderson**
Author & Former Presidential Candidate, American Party

BETRAYAL OF AMERICA

Bush's Appeasement of Communist Dictators Betrays American Principles

"An expert on the subject of no-win diplomacy who served during part of the Reagan administration as our Ambassador to Romania, tells about the betrayal of America. In his volume Ambassador Funderburk tells us that appeasement is leading America to an abattoir where liberty and freedom are slaughtered."

— **Meldrim Thomson, Jr.**
Former Governor of New Hampshire

"Ambassador David Funderburk is an American patriot of extraordinary courage, integrity, and discernment who represented the United States with great distinction as Ronald Reagan's Ambassador to Communist Romania . . . Instead of safeguarding U.S. national autonomy and defending the vital interests of our citizens, our government has rejected even a moral alliance with innocent people struggling for liberty in the Baltics, preferring instead to transfer our resources, our technology, and our moral capital to Marxist-Leninist despots in China, the USSR, and too many other places. Ambassador Funderburk provides an invaluable account which adds to his consistent far-sighted warnings regarding Communist deception and duplicity and the tragedy of our government's collaboration with the very forces which seek to deprive us of our freedom . . . It is a compelling account by one who has witnessed the betrayal of our nation by persons entrusted with its care."

— **Howard Phillips**
Chairman, The Conservative Caucus

"An outstanding book full of tangible evidence of the instrumentalities used by President Bush to promote the goals of a "New World Order.""

— **Andrew J. Gatsis**
Brigadier General, U.S. Army (Ret.)

"Many others among us know the players and know the score, but Ambassador Funderburk is one of the few with the courage, integrity, and patriotism to tell it like it was, and is, and to tell us, straight from the shoulder, what we can and must do about it."

— **Tom Anderson**
Author & Former Presidential Candidate, American Party